THE
GETTY KOUROS
COLLOQUIUM

Published by: KAPON EDITIONS - GREECE

Design: RACHEL MISDRACHI-KAPON

Translated by: ALEX DOUMAS
(pp. 25-26, 31-47, 51-52, 61-62)

Text edited by: ANGELIKI KOKKOU

Photographs by: LOUIS MELUSO

Artistic advisor: MOSES KAPON

Type-setting by: PHOTOGRAMMA Ltd.

Photographic reproductions: MICHAILIDES Bros

Stripping: G. PANOPOULOS

Printing: E. DANIEL & Co. S.A.

Printed in Athens, Greece, 1993

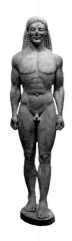

THE
GETTY KOUROS
COLLOQUIUM

THE J. PAUL GETTY MUSEUM

NICHOLAS P. GOULANDRIS FOUNDATION•MUSEUM OF CYCLADIC ART

Athens, 25-27 May 1992

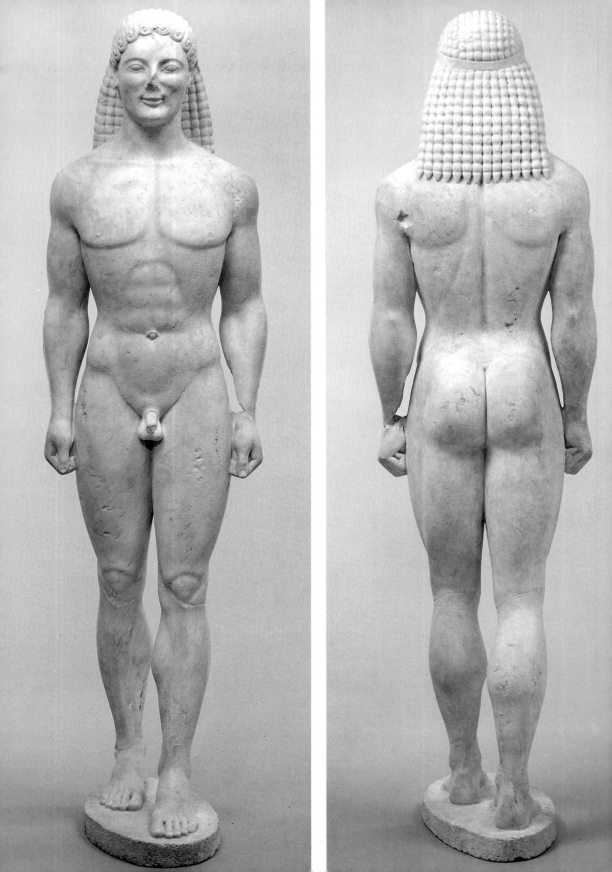

Dolly Goulandris

PREFACE

Now that the Getty Kouros Colloquium is over, and all the excitement of the kouros' arrival, and alas his departure for Malibu, gone, it is perhaps time to sit down and reminisce about what the results of this meeting represent.

It is the first time a Colloquium has been held for just one statue and, I believe, the first time so much research and study has been dedicated to one work of art. Furthermore, it is the first International Colloquium this Museum has organized.

The tone of the meeting was set by the opening remarks of Dr. Marion True. She stated quite openly and honestly the problems and her doubts, and presened all the relevant information; she then asked the international archaeologists present for their views.

The great achievement of the Colloquium, in my opinion, was the pervading spirit of friendship and camaraderie amongst the many specialists involved, despite their differences of opinion concerning the kouros.

As gesture of friendship and collaboration towards the Getty Museum, and the public in general who could not attend the meeting, we have decided to publish the papers given there.

All our thanks to Mr. Harold Williams and the Board of Trustees of the Getty Museum for their generous help in bringing over the kouros and for giving the Greek and European public the opportunity of viewing him for another two months.

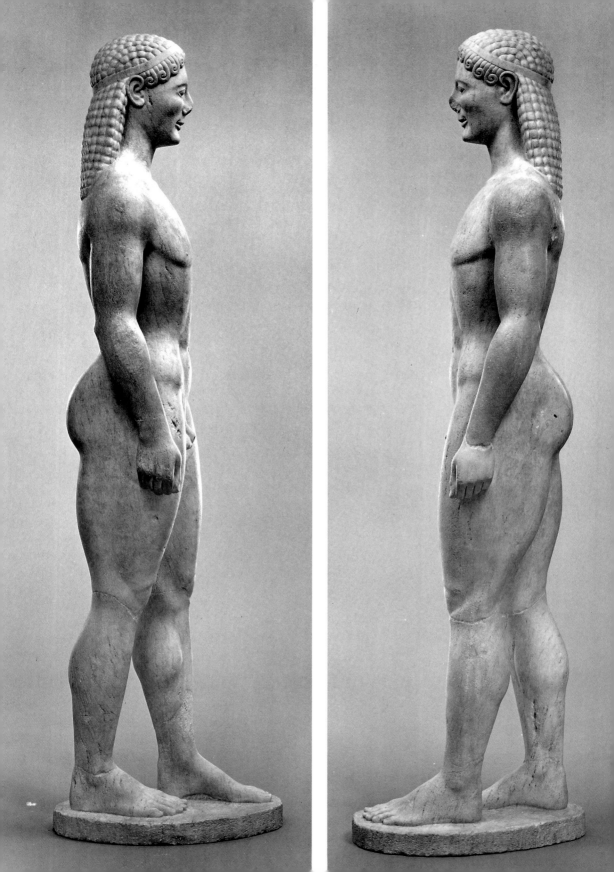

John Walsh
Director of the J. Paul Getty Museum

FOREWORD

The international colloquium on the Getty kouros held last year in Athens, of which this book is the record, was undertaken at the generous suggestion of Dolly Goulandris in order to give specialists the chance to debate this baffling statue. Many European experts on Greek sculpture had never seen the piece in the nine years since it came to light, so it was a further advantage to be able to exhibit it for several months at the Museum of Cycladic Art in Athens, where it could be compared with its nearby brothers (or distant ancestors).

The authenticity of the Getty kouros is no longer a problem for the Getty Museum alone. The newsworthy question may initially have been whether the Getty had acquired a great archaeological rediscovery or instead made an expensive mistake, but now, six years after the piece was first exhibited and published, its genuineness has become a question that affects the whole field. If genuine, it adds an impressive and beautifully preserved example (albeit with some curious anomalies) to the small group of authentic kouroi. If false, it is an astonishing recent creation, made with a rare combination of empathy, technical skill, and scientific knowledge by a faker whose other works must be very good indeed, and in fact may well have been bought by other museums.

As I write, the kouros is on display in Malibu with casts of the Tenea and Anavyssos kouroi in an exhibition designed to let visitors explore the still-unresolved question of its authenticity. After years of intensive research, we recognize that the puzzle may not be solved in our time. Our studies and those of our colleagues have nevertheless considerable value in themselves, and we are delighted to see them published. Professor Lambrinoudakis has our gratitude for having served as chairman of the colloquium. I am grateful above all to Mrs. Goulandris for organizing the project. Her openhanded hospitality made a deep impression on all who attended the colloquium. We are indebted to her and to the staff of her exemplary museum for producing this book with such speed and efficiency.

CONTENTS

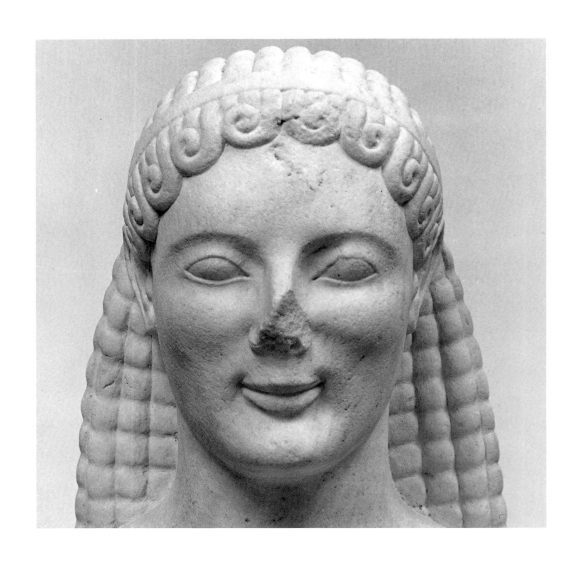

Marion True

THE GETTY KOUROS: BACKGROUND ON THE PROBLEM

The problem of the authenticity of the Getty kouros is an issue for our entire discipline. Do we include this statue in the corpus of known ancient kouroi, or do we relegate it to the growing class of masterful forgeries, created intentionally to deceive? And in making these judgements, what kinds of stylistic, technical and scientific information can be relied upon to assist us? Our intention in organizing this forum was to bring together scholars with a special interest in Archaic sculpture to present the results of recent research, to dispel some incorrect assumptions, and to air the widely varying opinions that have developed over five years since the statue was first publicly exhibited and published.

No aspect of the Getty kouros is straightforward. From the day, September 18, 1983, when it arrived in Malibu in seven pieces, it raised questions. Where was it found? As it was said to have been in a Swiss private collection for fifty years, why had it never been reassembled, though it was virtually complete? And what accounted from the strangely pale and floury appearance of the surface of the stone? Pursuing solutions to these questions only raised more. Basically the problems can be divided into three areas: the statue's seemingly anomalous combination of stylistic features, the unusual type of marble from which it is sculpted, and its problematic modern history.

Stylistic Anomalies

In terms of style, the figure appears unusually slender, narrow and rounded in the shoulders, small in the waist, and lacking the vitality and muscular tension one expects among the known kouroi. The treatment of the torso, front and back, is flat and schematic, as if the artist employed pure convention instead of real understanding of the anatomy. The curls around the forehead are thick and doughy, and from the back, the broad tresses of the hair seem to be divided into a too-regular grid.

The overall surface of the figure is oddly dull and floury, lacking the translucency we expect in Greek marble sculpture, and there are a number of obvious fissures in the marble. Most noticeable is the one in the center of the forehead, which must have been already evident to the sculptor when he was carving, as he modified the outline of the curl just to proper left of the central part. This use of a flawed stone for an Archaic statue seems unusual as other Archaic pieces were abandoned when flaws in the marble became apparent.

In its peculiar combination of anatomical features, the piece does not fit comfortably into the general chronological framework of stylistic development created by Gisela Richter. The wiglike hairstyle, in the number of strands and the gridlike regularity of its horizontal divisions, is closest to that found most often among kouroi of the very early Sounion Group, which are generally dated to the later seventh and early sixth centuries. The closest parallel for the simple and calligraphic sculpting of the hands, with the last joints of the little fingers turning in at right angles to the thighs, is found in the hands of the small Tenea kouros, now in Munich, dated around the second quarter of the sixth century. The Tenea kouros is also most similar to the Getty statue in its delicate proportions. Moving down to the feet, the parallels become later still. The regular oval plinth and the feet of the Getty kouros, which appear very naturalistic in their rendering, are most closely comparable to the feet associated with Kouros no. 12 from the Ptoon sanctuary or the feet attached to a base found on the Akropolis, both of which have been assigned to the Group of Anavyssos-Ptoon 12 and dated to the third quarter of the sixth century.

Thus, the comparisons for individual features cover the better part of a century. But while this seemingly anachronistic combination of features is problematic, it is not impossible in a work of ancient art. Parallels do exist for each feature, and other kouroi show similar odd combinations of seemingly early and late details.

Still, beyond the seemingly anachronistic combination of details, there is an unsettling feeling of familiarity when confronted with this statue. Its resemblance to the kouros from Anavyssos has been pointed out by many observers. Though closer comparison does indicate that this similarity is quite superficial, the lingering suggestion of imitation is not easy to dismiss.

Since the Getty statue does not fall comfortably into a previously defined chronological group, we had to consider the possibility of identifying regional style. Valuable studies have defined characteristics for a number of regional styles, but unfortunately, the Getty kouros does not fit comfortably into any one of these. Its closest parallels connect it to works from various areas, most notably Attica, Boeotia, and perhaps Corinth.

The Marble

One feature that we hoped might have proved helpful in identifying the place of manufacture of the Getty kouros was the material from which it is carved. But its marble presented another puzzle. Scientific analysis identified the stone as Thasian dolomitic marble, probably from a quarry on the northeast corner of the island. The use of Thasian marble is not unknown in the Archaic period, but there is as yet no real evidence for its widespread exportation in the Archaic period. Known pieces that are made from Thasian stone have either been found on Thasos or nearby sites like Samothrace, or originally came from Thasos. Also, as the marble-rich island of Paros dominated Thasos politically from the early seventh century onward, we should expect to find some features that could be called Parian if this figure were carved on the island of Thasos. These features are not present.

During the process of analyzing the marble, we turned to the geologists to see if there were any method of analyzing the weathered surface of the stone to confirm the sculpture's age. Because the stone was almost pure dolomite, the alteration layer offered some hope. Evidence for the naturally occurring process of dedolomitization appeared to be present, and scientific expertise suggested that it could not be artificially induced. At last, we seemed to have a reliable, objective criterion on which to base an opinion for the statue's authenticity. However, doubts about this evidence too have now been raised by the discovery that the alteration layer is actually calcium oxalate, which is not the result of dedolomitization but the result, instead, of the interaction of the dolomitic marble with oxalic acid. Oxalic acid may be produced by naturally growing lichens; it is also used by artists and forgers for cleaning stone.

Modern History

The last issue is the statue's lack of any established provenance. The statue was imported into the United States from Switzerland in 1983, accompanied by documents that claimed it had been in the collection of Dr. Jean Lauffenburger of Geneva since the 1930's. Photocopies of letters to Dr. Lauffenburger suggested that it had been seen by a variety of people, including the great scholar of Greek sculpture, Professor Ernst Langlotz.

Unfortunately, when we tried to procure the originals of these letters, we were told they had disappeared. Then, when these photocopies were subjected to the scrutiny of a German expert in typewriters, postal codes and other means of verification, they proved to be cleverly manufactured composites. The Langlotz letter in particular could be shown to be a forgery because, though the letter is dated 1952, the postal code on the letter head did not come into existence until 1972. The association with the Lauffenburger collections thus appears to have been a clever hoax, and the real modern history of the statue prior to 1983 remains a mystery.

The Discovery of the Fake Torso and the Reevaluation of the Getty Kouros

In April 1990, the whole story took an interesting twist when Dr. Jeffery Spier of London telephoned to say that he had finally found the piece of evidence that would prove our kouros to be a fake. Together, we went to Basel, Switzerland, and saw the small torso of a kouros.

Though undoubtedly a fake, this piece did show some disturbing similarities to our kouros, especially in the rounded, sloping treatment of the shoulders and upper arms, the volume of the chest, the schematic rendering of the hands, and the shape and size of the genitals. The entire surface had been bathed in acid, then crudely patinated with an iron oxide.

The owner of the torso allowed me to take some small chips of stone from one of the broken surfaces for marble analysis. Two samples were tested independently, and proved that the stone of this piece was also Thasian dolomitic marble. Recognizing that this torso was a valuable piece of evidence in our effort to unravel the story of the Getty kouros – a piece of evidence that might well be destroyed – the Getty Museum purchased it in August 1990 as a forgery for study purposes. Dr. Spier published his discovery and conclusions in the *Burlington Magazine* of September 1990 in his article, "Blinded by Science."

Once in possession of the torso, we learned that a head had once existed for this piece. It was with a dealer in Geneva who donated it to the Museum so the figure could be reassembled. The head actually helped us to reconstruct the history of the fake. The forgery is said to have been made in Rome around 1984-1985, reportedly by a man named Fernando Onore. The head, which is of a completely different color than the torso, preserves the original pale appearance of the entire statue. It was broken off when the dealers realized they could not sell the piece as genuine, and the body was repatinated to give a more persuasive appearance. Clearly, this effort did not work too well since the new color could not disguise the ravages of the acid bath.

As Dr. Spier wrote in his article, market gossip reported that the small kouros and the Getty statue were made from the same block of stone by the same sculptor. Dr. Spier also reported to us that both were patinated by a second craftsman, not the forger, and that this individual had given him a recipe for the creation of the patina of the Getty kouros.

Possession of both the torso and the head gave us at the Getty the opportunity to investigate these rumors and to try to discover their truthfulness. It also gave us the opportunity to review all of the work that had been done some five years earlier, to see what mistakes, if any, might have been made in the original analysis and what new advances in scholarship might help with these problems. In this reexamination, our perspective was reversed from the first efforts – this time, we were prepared to prove that our kouros was a fake.

Thus far, however, we have been unsuccessful. Analysis of the stone has shown that the Getty kouros and the fake torso could not have come from the same block, and most likely, not even from the same quarry source. Extensive technical examinations of both pieces have shown that the sculpting techniques used on the two pieces are dramatically different: while the small fake preserves the obvious marks of modern power tools, the large statue has revealed no tool marks inconsistent with ancient Archaic sculpting techniques. And comparison of the two alteration layers shows a marked contrast: the surface of the fake has been produced by a simple acid bath while the other is far more complex. Every effort to reproduce the recipe that Dr. Spier was given has failed and as yet, it has not been possible to replicate the surface of our statue in a laboratory.

What we are continuing to investigate is the relationship between the torso and the Getty statue. Though they are apparently not by the same hand or from the same block, they do seem to be related. In terms of chronology, it is possible that photographs of our kouros may have been available to the forger of the small torso. It is also possible that the forger had access at some point to our statue.

During our seven years of work on this piece, we have tried to pursue every possible avenue of research to learn the truth. One of the most obvious suggestions was made to us first by Bernard Holtzmann, who asked if we had ever looked at the statue outside in natural sunlight. In April 1992, the Getty kouros was placed in the courtyard of the conservation laboratory at the Museum, under the unforgiving sunlight of a perfect California day. In truth, the statue came together as a convincing unity in these conditions; its peculiar combination of anomalous features was suddenly less disconcerting, and the subtlety of the rendering of so many minor features gave me a renewed respect for the skill of the sculptor. But the question remains, was this sculptor an Archaic Greek artisan or an inspired and knowledgeable forger?

Cynics have asked, if this statue is good enough to perplex the professionals, does it really matter if it is genuine or not? It does indeed matter, because fakes distort the record of our cultural history and, once included in the corpus of accepted genuine works of art, can plague generations of students and scholars. But ethical considerations of forgery are a larger issue. As Professor John Merryman wrote recently in his article on "Counterfeit Art":

"Counterfeit works of art are themselves authentic cultural objects whose study can tell us something about their producers and about ourselves. But until they are correctly identified and labeled and removed from circulation they can only mislead, misinform, and misrepresent." (*International Journal of Cultural Properties* I, 1992, p. 35).

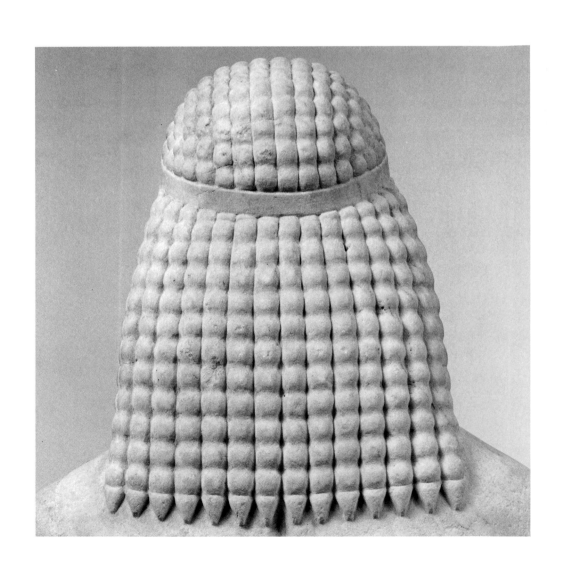

Brunilde Sismondo-Ridgway

IN DEFENSE OF AUTHENTICITY

First of all, I cannot firmly state that I know the Getty kouros is genuine. If anybody knows with certainty that it is a forgery, I believe he or she has a moral obligation to come forward and say so. As John Walsh has said, this is not a Getty problem, but a problem for all scholars working with ancient art. So far, each "accusation" I have heard has attributed the statue to a different forger.

The existence of a faked kouros is not, *per se,* proof against the Getty statue. The two pieces look very different; I am told the marble, although Thasian, is from a different vein; the attempts at aging the surface of the fake were made with identifiable agents; the anatomical treatment is different (except perhaps for the hands); feet and plinth are omitted in the forgery, whereas they are present for scrutiny in the Getty kouros. The level of knowledge exhibited by the sculptor of the attested fake is considerably lower.

With the Getty kouros, we have reached an impasse; if some details can be paralleled in genuine kouroi, they are assumed to have been copied from that specific source, but unparalleled details are taken as indication of forgery – the sculptor did not know any better.

I find the following renderings relevant. The Getty knee is anomalous, with one continuous curve to the muscle above the patella, rather than the two separate sections typical of most kouroi and truer to nature. Yet this pattern finds comparison in a leg in the Thasos Museum, and in a Delian kouros, A 4084. This latter statue, the Kroisos, Akr. 665, and the Getty kouros share the peculiarity of having the inner outline of the forearm reflect, in negative as it were, the outer contour of the adjacent thigh. This is a technical detail not immediately obvious, especially since the statue in Delos is little known and poorly illustrated. It would not be represented even in a very rich cast collection. The plinth of the Getty kouros has an equally unusual form (a *lectio diffici-lior*). Although it could have been copied from that of Ptoon 12 or Akr. 665 (surprising holdings for a cast collection; the forger would have needed to be in Greece), Dr. Kleemann has shown that the positioning of the feet is not the same.

Feet are a most difficult part of an ancient statue. The transition from arch to plinth surface is handled in different ways by different carvers (cf. the various kouroi in the

National Museum). The forger could have avoided this problem by omitting the feet. (I cannot accept the argument that the value of the piece would have been considerably diminished by this omission; the Cleveland kouros, which was cited as an example, lacks not only feet but also its head, a more important detail.) In rendering the smallest toe turned inward toward the other toes, the Getty sculptor reveals a deep understanding of Late Archaic foot forms.

Again, unusual knowledge is revealed by the asymmetries noticeable when the statue

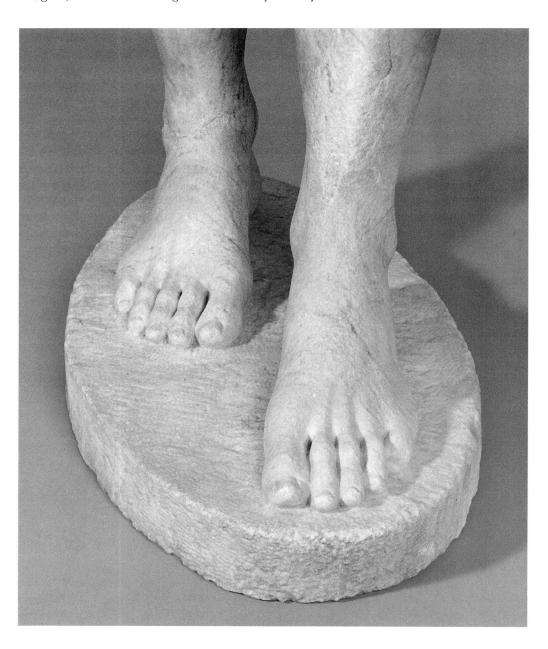

is viewed from above; comparable asymmetries appear in the Kroisos, as shown in an unpublished photograph. A cast collection would certainly include the Kroisos, but I doubt that photography from above, which requires special equipment, would have been allowed indiscriminately, or would even have been considered necessary by the forger. The front and back planes of the Getty kouros' torso meet on the sides along a faint ridge, visible in photographs taken before the arms were reattached, but not very noticeable at present. Just such a ridge exists in several, though by no means in all, kouroi at the National Museum – most obvious in the torso from Megara, but also in Ptoon 10 etc. The most disturbing feature of the Getty kouros is its "dead" surface; yet a comparably dull appearance is presented by the Keratea kouros.

Individual details of the Getty kouros can be matched, but the chronological range implied by them is too wide, it has been said, and thus makes the statue eclectic. Yet equally "eclectic" statues have been found in controlled excavations; the Motya Youth may serve as extreme example, although I do not believe the Getty kouros could be Magna Graecian. Some genuine kouroi show similar range. The kouros from the east pediment of the temple of Apollo at Delphi has a pointed epigastric arch and a lack of abdominal partitions that belie its date after 513. The still-unpublished Merenda kouros has "early" eyes, a very pointed epigastric arch, but naturalistic fists with staggered fingers, and hair swelling in the back under the fillet. The bronze Piraeus Apollo combines "late" feet with "early" anatomy and face. Perhaps we should not assign strict chronological values to specific renderings, as Richter's system of classification has encouraged us to do.

It has been pointed out that no traces of paint appear on the Getty kouros, in contrast to others. Would such paint appear under the calcium layer? Do all kouroi reveal painted details? (I understand the Melos kouros may not.) It has been said that the plinth of the Getty kouros could never have been set into a base; yet Phrasikleia has retained her plinth intact. Photographs taken at discovery show her and her mate with rings of lead near their feet; another photo gives Phrasikleia's base with the lead still in place. Would traces of lead be revealed by microscopic examination? Do we have plinths from pedimental kouroi (e.g., Delphi)? They may not have been embedded in the pedimental floor, but just rested on the surface.

Looking at genuine kouroi from a comparative point of view has made me realize how "peculiar" and individual they appear. The hair rendering (back) of the Munich kouros is unique. The Tenea kouros looks different from all others. Delos A 1742 has a four-faceted right, a three-faceted left hand, showing that patterns may change from one side of the same statue to the other, perhaps as a result of experimentation (as in Archaic architecture).

Forgeries need time to be detected. Works by Dossena would not mislead us, yet they deceived contemporary scholars. Some authentic pieces can still be doubted today: the New York kouros, the Berlin kore. Let us not forget that even Kroisos was initially thought to be a fake. Perhaps 50 years from now we shall see the Getty kouros in its true light. The Colloquium has highlighted for me the gaps in my own knowledge, at the same time enriching it considerably. I have never profited so much from a scholarly meeting, and I am impressed by the atmosphere of objectivity, openness and friendliness in which it took place.

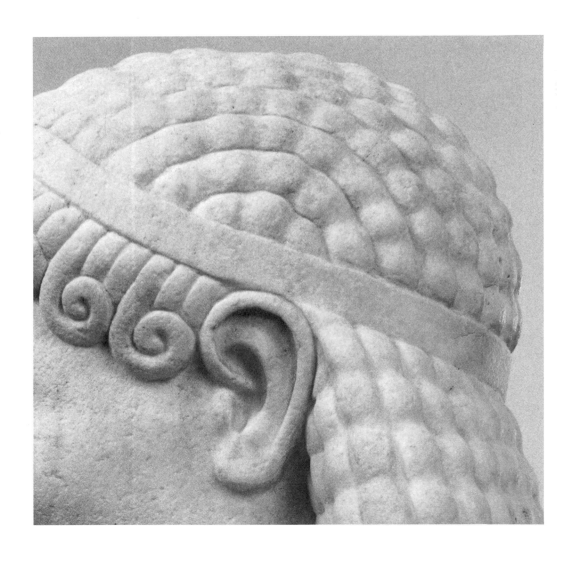

Evelyn B. Harrison

REMARKS ON THE STYLE OF THE GETTY KOUROS

It seems right that so many scholars make up the panel on the style of the Getty kouros. Style in itself is a complex matter, for there are many kinds of styles, and in evaluating style we also have to consider iconography, what a work represents, for whom it was made, and how to read it in the language of its time. In all this, chronology is of the first importance. Unfortunately, the one thing that no one can doubt about the Getty kouros is that there has been concealment of evidence for its chronology. This is an impediment that we all have to face.

We approach the kouros from various directions. I belong to the excavation archaeologists. We have never dug up a whole kouros in the Athenian Agora. My job has been to look for parallels for the pieces that we find and to try to visualize a whole kouros on the basis of these parallels. To any scholar confronted with an object for the first time, the initial overall impression is important, but because of my experience I tend to move on quickly to examining details.

In January 1985, when I first met the kouros, he was lying on his back in the basement, assembled but not yet glued together. I had never been shown any photographs, and the sight was not at all what I expected. Let me try to explain.

From a report by Stanley Margolis I knew that the statue was made of dolomitic marble. The only dolomitic sculptor's marble that I knew was Thasian. I had encountered a lot of this in the Agora in sculptures of the Roman period but never in anything earlier than the time of Trajan, to which this portrait bust can be dated by its shape and style. The overall effect here is that of work in some stone harder than marble. Since this stone is unfriendly to soft modulation and fine detail, it is not surprising that it was not exported to central and southern Greek cities in the Archaic and Classical periods. Corinth shows the same pattern as Athens. Perhaps it was only when imperial Roman taste came to dominate the Greek world that the Athenians allowed this marble to compete with their own.

Because the Getty kouros was of dolomitic marble, I expected it to show the style of the north Aegean, or, if the stone came from some more exotic source, that the style would be still more unusual.

This turned out not to be the case. What I saw really did seem to be the familiar Thasian marble, but, instead of recalling Archaic works from Thasos, the kouros looked strangely like some well-known Boeotian and Attic kouroi, none of which has yet been found to be made of Thasian marble. At the same time, the kouros did not give the impression of being something old; somehow it looked new.

Why was this? It may have been partly the quality of the breaks. Those in the right arm were said to be recent, those in the left arm ancient, but to the naked eye they did not suggest a difference of 2,500 years.

Starting from the head down, I thought that the curls over the forehead looked unpleasantly doughy. They have neither the chisel-cut subdivisions into strands of the curls of the Anavyssos and Ptoon 12 kouroi nor the snail-shell-like plasticity of the big curls of the kouros from Kea. A flaw in the marble interfered with the carving of a curl over the center of the forehead; it was left flat and rough. Indeed, such flaws appear all over the statue; this was not a good piece of marble.

The collarbones are boringly understated, with slight relief and no verve to their curves. The pectorals are flat and depressed, almost inorganic in their shallow, uniform convexity, contrasting oddly with the developed and strongly modelled forms of the *rectus abdominis.*

The knees, too, are stiffly carved, inorganic and almost ugly. I know of no exact parallel. The feet are not unlike those assigned to the Ptoon 12 kouros, but the plinth does not look Archaic. Its simple oval and generous margin all around, the substantial thickness and clean rectangular edges, and the smooth horizontal trimming with a claw chisel recall Roman plinths made to be set on top of their bases rather than leaded into them.

When the kouros stands upright, the flat depressed pectorals are even more disturbing, especially in profile. In the front view the upper arms attached to the narrow sloping shoulders seem squeezed against the sides. Contrast the freely hanging arms of other kouroi, be they fat or thin.

The long hair in back conforms closely to that of the New York kouros, even to the fourteen strands. Four kouroi of the Sounion Group have this number, but it is extremely rare later on. Apparently our artist is selectively retrospective.

The hanging hair forms a rigid mass, not flat like the hair of the Sounion Group nor pliant like that in later works. Its meeting with the neck and shoulders is an intersection of solid forms, each independent of the other. This recalls sculpture of the twentieth century.

A close view of the face reveals no sharp edges anywhere. Traces of the abrasive finishing cut across the edges of the forms, dampening them down rather than following and enhancing them. Was this statue never meant to be painted?

We come to iconography: what was the statue meant to represent and for whom was it made? Andrew Stewart explains that kouroi in general embody the aristocratic ideal of physical and moral beauty. He quotes Theognis of Megara to show that the message is "replete with homosexual innuendo," and goes on to say, "a glance at the new Getty kouros underlines a point: a better commentary on the varied satisfactions offered by it and its fellows can hardly be imagined."

Stewart's association of the Getty kouros with Megara is born of disinformation, and his "glance" has failed to take in the crudeness of its contrasts. There is homosexual appeal in this kouros as well as in the others that Stewart calls its fellows, but their youthful androgyny is a not-yet-differentiated whole rather than an abrupt juxtaposition of contradictory elements.

We can see how contradictory these elements are in the ancient Greek view of young male beauty when we compare Aristophanes' listing in the *Clouds* of the happy results to be expected from the old-style education: a well-nourished chest, bright skin, big shoulders, short speech, big buttocks and a small penis. The Getty kouros has the last two, but his chest and shoulders are the opposite of the ideal. Why his skin is so dull we must leave to our technical colleagues to explain if they can.

The manner of combining male and female in the Getty kouros seems to be modern: it finds a dramatic parallel in the Athena Parthenos created by Alan Lequire for the Parthenon in Nashville. Lequire has explained that he conceives of the goddess Athena as a combination of male and female; to express this he has made the head masculine and the body feminine. By comparison, the Getty kouros with his girlish face and apologetic shoulders looks harmless and ingratiating. Like his ancient cousins he seems designed to please a wealthy client, but in the modern manner.

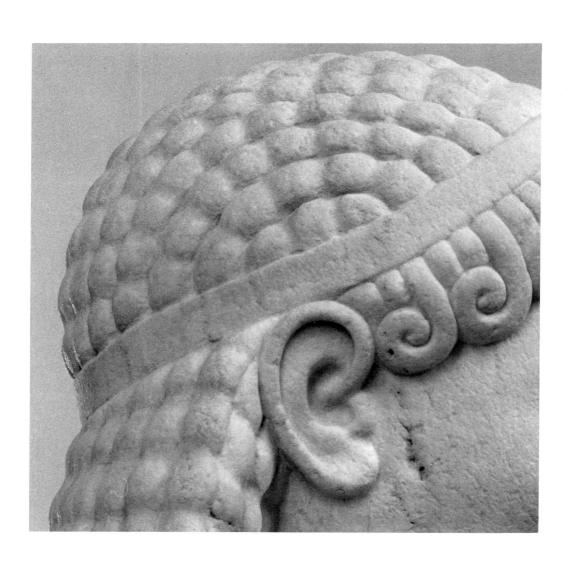

Bernard Holtzmann

A CONTRIBUTION TO THE ATHENS COLLOQUIUM
ON THE GETTY KOUROS

The Getty kouros, although undoubtedly of Thasian marble from the Vathy region, bears no stylistic relation to the few fragmentary kouroi that have been found on Thasos: these, just like the korai, exhibit a mixture of Ionian influences – Cycladic and Aeolian in varying degrees – while the Getty kouros is clearly atticizing. This being so, if it is thought unlikely that a Thasian sculptor joined the Attic school, it is even more improbable that an Athenian sculptor came to work on Thasos. In sculpture, Athens was essentially at the receiving end during the 6th century and her influence is not attested outside the regions bordering on Attica: Boeotia, Megaris and Corinthia.

However, this lack of accord between the style and the marble is not enough to warrant the conclusion that the Getty kouros is a forgery: we still know very little about the diffusion of marbles in the Archaic period. Even so, it is a fact that the marbles available at the time were very few and that Thasian marble was one of them. Vitruvius (X, 2, 15) mentions that the Ephesians had considered importing marble from Paros, Thasos, Proconnesus and Heracleia for the construction of the temple of Artemis in around 560; furthermore, the Ludovisi-Boston thrones, made in 470-460, are of Thasian marble and their provenance is generally placed in south Italy. If, therefore, a Cycladic or very cycladicizing sculptor in about 460 was able, on the coast of Locri, to carve works in marble, from Thasos, one cannot *a priori* rule out the possibility that a very atticizing sculptor was able, in central Greece in about 530-520, to carve a kouros in Thasian marble. A systematic analysis of the marble of the Archaïc sculptures in the National Museum of Athens and the Acropolis Museum would perhaps reveal a much more complex reality than that proposed by Lepsius a century ago. Until Pentelic marble came to the fore in the second half of the 5th c., Attic sculptures and, even more, those from the neighbouring regions were carved from a variety of different marbles.

Moreover, is it possible that the flaws visible on the right side of the kouros – in front of the ear and on the flank, upper thigh, leg and ankle – could have been produced over a period of no more than thirty years, since modern quarrying of Thasian marble dates back only to the fifties? They are in any case similar to those exhibited by sculptures that have been buried for a very long time in the Thasian earth.

As far as the style is concerned, it is clear that the Getty kouros fits badly into Richter's chronological system (its date diminishes from the head to the feet!) and Langlotz's geographical scheme (a general Attic appearance, with isolated insular features and an overall very graphic style); also certain details (the flatness of the torso between the pectorals and clavicles, the schematic outline of the fingers and the too rectilinear line of the buttock cleavage) appear weak and thus suspect. But would not similar defects be found in most of the kouroi, if they were to be subjected to an equally suspicious review? These disparities in date, style and execution hardly seem sufficient to challenge the overall probability that the work is authentic. Has not every discovery made in recent years, whether it be the bronze kouros from Piraeus, the Mozia ephebe or the colossal kouros on Samos, brought into question what we believed was established fact? In these circumstances, would it not be methodologically safer to adopt the principle of the philologists, who, faced with two textual variants, constrain themselves to choose the *lectio difficilior* rather than reject out of hand something new and inconvenient in the name of ideas whose systematization schematizes and impoverishes the complex reality which they claim to expound on the basis of a few works? In the absence of hard evidence of forgery – strong enough, that is, to outweigh the *a priori* improbability of a contemporary forger, otherwise unknown, possessing such a mastery of ancient techniques and styles; and the Colloquium has not produced such a proof – the Getty kouros should receive the benefit of the doubt and be considered as a genuine ancient work. In the present state of things – the frailty of stylistic judgements; the tentativeness of scientific analytical techniques – only a detective type of investigation might perhaps be able to find the solution to the problem. It is strange that this approach has apparently not been explored in six years.

John Boardman

CRITERIA

I do not know the age of the Getty kouros, but it seems to pose important problems of confidence in the criteria we employ, which I explore here briefly, without becoming involved in specifics. Three areas of uncertainty are involved. One is its recent history, which ought to be a matter of fact and might be decisive. One is judgement of physical analysis by scientists, which ought to be decisive, but manifestly is not. One is judgement of style, which is highly subjective although not completely so, since in many areas of stylistic judgement there is general scholarly consensus. Spier's paper has raised the question of recent history, in this case still open to debate, and inasmuch as it too in some degree depends on stylistic judgement about the kouros' brother it will remain vague until convincing documentary evidence is forthcoming. Scientific evidence may seem conflicting, though we should not abandon placing reliance on its findings, and they need interpretation no less than do stylistic judgements. Spier encourages us to have more faith in our own stylistic judgement, but then we are bound to ask whose judgement, since we have to examine the credentials of the judge no less than we should of any scientist and the methods he or she applies. So this is a brief personal reflection on personal experience of examination of authenticity, based on experience with the Getty kouros.

I first saw the kouros in photographs; then in Malibu, where the conservator convinced me that in the eyes of science it was ancient. My initial reaction was an instinctive one. Instinct without experience is useless; so what this means is that my instinct depended entirely on my previous experience not only of kouroi but of Greek art in general. It should be possible, although extremely difficult, to explain such instinctive judgements in terms of definable knowledge and demonstrable parallels, visual and otherwise. Inadequate experience of kouroi would disqualify me, just as would inadequate experience of other areas of Greek art and archaeology. So this is a matter of self-analysis, itself also subjective.

I had seen many kouroi without studying any in very great depth. Facing the kouros I saw that its surface was strange, but understood how that might have happened in ways that need not call its authenticity into question. I was perhaps overpersuaded by scientific arguments that I could not adequately judge. I have used science, have learned to understand some of the ways in which it can deceive, but was in general ready to accept views that seemed reasonable and based on arguments that I could more or less understand. I refer in this case particularly to scientific arguments directed to age and exposure of surfaces and breaks. There is also the question of scientific analysis of composition. I have had sufficient experience of the early days of clay analysis to know how disastrously inadequate such a study can be until an adequate databank of comparative material is available. For clay the situation is by now, after 25 years, considerably improved but far from perfect. For stone, and indeed metals, even with isotope analyses, the situation remains quite primitive and open to controlled scepticism. One might also have faith in one's eye for marbles – but how has that eye been trained and on what secure data?

But what of style? There were no individual features that seemed wrong, but the ensemble was somehow awkward. There was no notable disparity in technical treatment between the parts – a useful criterion in other media, especially vase-painting – so I was reacting subconsciously to the feeling that in some way there was a discrepancy in an ensemble that presented this sort of hair, profile, proportion, anatomical detail etc. This view depended both on my knowledge of other kouroi, which was incomplete, but perhaps more importantly on my interpretation of my knowledge of other kouroi.

Did I, for example, follow those who believed that there were good stylistic grounds for discerning criteria for many local schools. On the whole I had little faith in such criteria except for a few obvious and small groups, like the Early Attic, where the criteria could be more readily defined in specific terms of hairstyle, anatomical patterning etc. And I justified this to myself by reflecting on the necessary mobility of sixth-century marble sculptors, not tied to a single workshop with a brisk daily production like a pottery, and the comparatively restricted areas in which they could learn and exercise their craft – principally on the marble islands themselves, in a period when other marble sources in Greece were yet to be exploited. The medium and techniques were difficult too, and the products far less susceptible to close analysis than the products of, say, the potter. This made kouroi far more personal and to some degree unpredictable products. In other words, my instinctive unease did not predispose me to condemn the kouros. Indeed, I deliberately went to the pictures in Miss Richter, and looked at many authentic kouroi asking myself how I would react to them if they appeared without documentation on the market today. Several failed the test. To put it crudely, many kouroi seemed stylistically disorganised or internally inconsistent, and I was unwilling to condemn a new one on such grounds alone, unless the inconsistencies were impossibly blatant.

Technical grounds could be decisive, especially if there was blatant discrepancy, which there is not. Our views on technique depend wholly on what we see and interpret, both processes being insecure since the condition of many marbles leaves technique obscure, and interpretation depends on what we know to be, or are told by others to be, possible. We readily fall into the trap of thinking that X could only happen after a certain date or in a certain place, when all we mean is that no one has yet recognised it earlier or elsewhere.

So what arguments will persuade me? A photograph of the statue being made would do the trick. For the science, I am inclined more to caution those who believe the results unquestioningly, than the scientists themselves, whom I have generally found to be modest and reasonable people. Yet these are matters where the interpretation cannot be left to them alone. And what of style? I will not be impressed by those who find there are incompatible mixtures here. I am a little more disposed to listen to those who find chronological inconsistencies, since these might be more clearly quantifiable. But I have little faith in the conventional dating, relative or absolute, of Archaic sculpture with the degree of precision that it is often given. Sculptors are likely to have responded more slowly and irregularly to novelty than more prolific and less ambitious craftsmen, and I have no reason to believe in closely knit packages of stylistic elements that should always go together in a given period or place. Real doubts about stylistic judgement can be exercised in periods when we imagine we have a far fuller understanding of date and origin, but the subject area of kouroi is surely not one in which we should feel any greater confidence. The kouros asks us to look at what grounds we have for confidence in our own judgement as much as it appeals to us for a view on its date.

The final question, I suppose, is "does it matter?" It matters only if the kouros is allowed to influence our judgement of the making of kouroi in Archaic Greece, which it seems not to, to any serious degree, and it seems to have had no significant archaeological context. It matters a great deal to those who own archaeological context. It matters a great deal to those who own it. And, I suppose, it matters a great deal to the self-esteem of those who feel that their scholarly integrity or expertise is on trial; but I sincerely hope that this is not an issue at all.

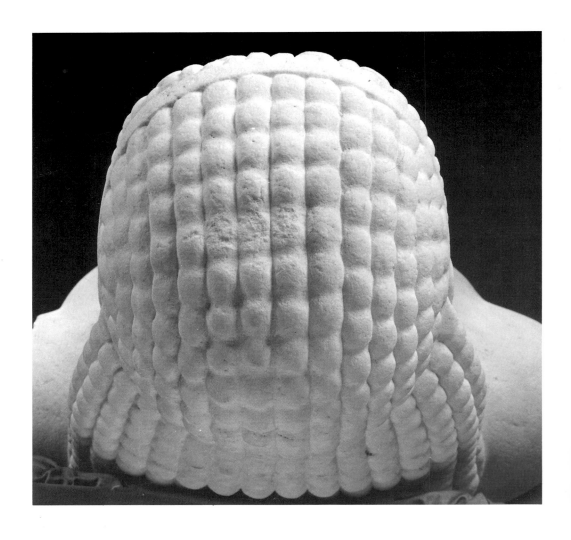

Vassilis Lambrinoudakis

SOME OBSERVATIONS ON THE AUTHENTICITY
OF THE GETTY KOUROS

To express an opinion on the authenticity of the Getty kouros is not an easy task. Its proportions are completely within the measurements known from genuine works, its stance and its well-studied organic movement are rendered with consistency, and most of the partial characteristics of its body seem to be well placed in the years of the Anavyssos-Ptoon 12 Group. Even the hairstyle, which adds a pronounced Archaic element to the figure, could theoretically be produced in Late Archaic times. Beads are common in this period and triangular tips occur on statues of the last quarter of the 6th century B.C. (Richter Nr. 169). The number of 16/14 tresses and the form of the curls on the forehead are equally attested on late kouroi (Richter Nrs. 116, 120, 154).

However, though study of the statue's component elements may reveal a consistency, our experience of known works of the period still troubles us when confronting it as a whole. The consequences of the unease are scepticism concerning its material and workmanship, as well as difficulties in the definition of the style and attribution to a specific artistic current. Beside other important remarks, here are listed some more observations pertaining to these problems.

The damage to the forehead as well as cavities elsewhere on the surface of the statue are explained in different ways. M. True noticed that the central part of the curls above the forehead had originally been reworked as a result of the crevice there. It seems that the same happened at the upper end of the groove rendering the spine, through which runs a fissure. This is the more probable explanation of the strange end of the groove, which cuts deep and almost vertically on the kouros' right side in the marble under the curls. The two cases show that the sculptor deliberately used a defective material, trying to conceal some imperfections but tolerating others. This is not the normal attitude of the Archaic sculptor.

Some elements of the Getty statue seem to exclude the possibility of synthesis of progressive and conservative elements or of local taste observed in Late Archaic times: (a) The strong structuring in the abdominal area, similar to that of the Anavyssos kouros, is difficult to reconcile with the flat chest, the more refined proportions and the shallowness of the upper torso, which display a more uniform and schematic concept of

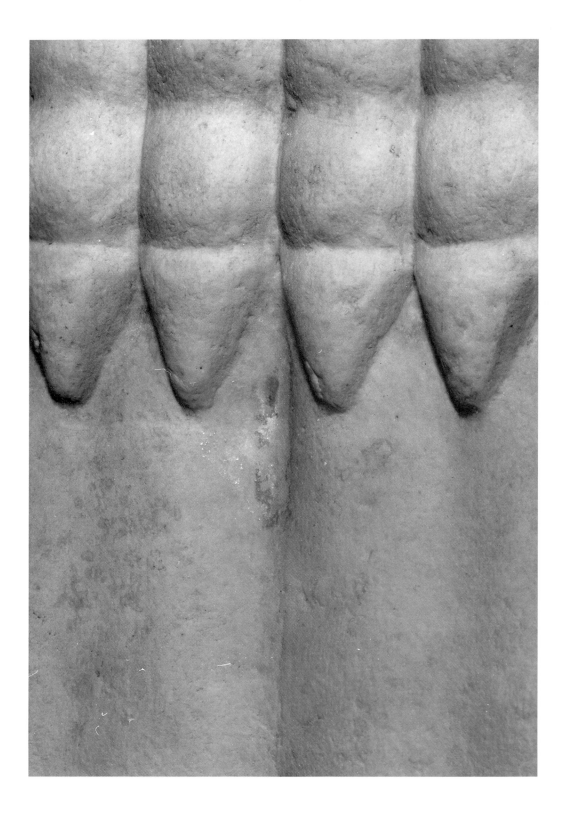

the body, such as one sees in the Kea and the Ptoon 12 statues. The failure becomes evident in comparison with the Kea kouros, a genuine synthesis of the two directions, in which the clear structure of the abdomen has been absorbed within the uniform scheme of the body. (b) The vertical separation of the buttocks is at variance with the sense of movement existing in the rest of the statue. (c) The hair falls with a stiffness unknown in the time of the Anavyssos kouros, its beads have a distinctly independent outline, as was the case much earlier, and the arrangement of the tresses in groups on the crown returns to the rough language of differentiation of the first kouroi, no longer apparent in Late Archaic compositions. While in the latter (for ex. Anavyssos, Ptoon 12) the differentiation of the bead tresses is influenced by the more naturalistic way by treatment of the hair, the Getty kouros shows a rough distinction of a group of four tresses to the left and two to the right of the parting achieved by interruption of the transverse axes of the beads.

The appearance of the evidently fake kouros recently acquired by the Getty Museum seems to support the doubts about the authenticity of the Getty kouros. The faker sought to render the period and the style represented by the latter; his work is nearer to the Anavyssos kouros than the Getty statue itself (wider face, narrower and concave outline of hair, whose ends form a curve on the back without triangular tips, plastic modelling of chest and shoulders), but on the other hand it selects decorative elements from other contemporary statues (shape of spiral curls on the forehead inspired by the kouros of Ptoon 12, their double alignment borrowed from heads like Richter Nrs. 142, 143 and 148) and reproduces the oddest characteristic of the Getty kouros, i.e. the hair pattern. The analogies in eclecticism between the fake and the Getty kouros, the much less skillful reproduction by the former of the most uncommon feature of the latter (the hair), and the affinity of their unusual material seem to connect the circumstances in which both statues were produced.

The question of authenticity of the Getty kouros cannot be answered in a satisfactory way by the means we have available today. If the evidence against its genuineness were stronger, one could more easily support that it was created by a very skillful modern sculptor who drew his inspiration from statues such as the Anavyssos kouros (abdominal area, waist and hips, forearms, sloping shoulders, thighs and calves), the Kea kouros (hairstyle, oval face, flat chest, deeper abdomen, narrower hips, musculature of the back, combination of narrower chest and laterally voluminous buttoks) and the Ptoon 12 kouros (long face, refined proportions, rigid hair, feet), but also from earlier works, such as the kouroi of the Sounion Group (treatment of the beads) and the Ptoon 10 kouros (convex outline of hair behind).

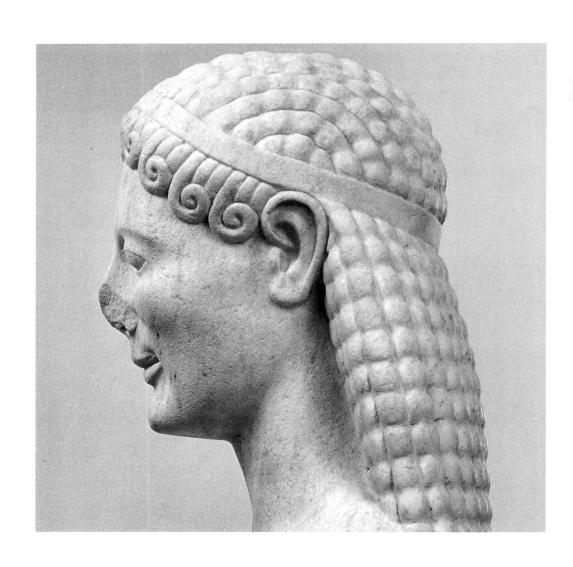

Jean Marcadé

AN HONEST OPINION ABOUT THE GETTY KOUROS

O f all the kouroi known, the kouros of the Paul Getty Museum is undoubtedly the most appealing to modern taste, the most balanced, the most elegant. Slender, with pleasing proportions, a slim waist half way between the broadening of the torso at the level of the chest and the corresponding broadening of the pelvis on the upper thigh: from the front it brings to mind the ideal figure for a beauty competition; the long swelling legs and the rather feminine sweetness of the expression add to its charm.

The Archaic conventions have been used with ease, particular significance being attached to design, for even on the lateral face below the waist the modelling is less well studied than the design. Indeed the design displays an abundance of echoes and correspondences. The straight line formed by the clavicles heralds the horizontal divisions of the *rectus abdominis major*. The curved lines of the pectorals are repeated in reverse on a smaller scale on the folds above the patella. The thoracic arch is recalled by the arched depression underlining the abdomen. On the back, the shoulder blades correspond in shape to the pectorals, the oblique end of the dorsals corresponds to the two edges of the thoracic arch, lastly, the spinal groove corresponds to the *linea alba*. As far as the lateral face is concerned, the volume of the hair announces the swelling of the thighs behind, and so on.

The accomplished draughtsmanship of the head, on which the eyes, the mouth, the ears and the hair constitute equally attractive features, is even more pronounced: e.g. the line of the edge of the eye socket, the opening of the eyelids in which the eyeball curves, the arc of the mouth between the prominent cheeks and the pointed chin, which give the profile an air of irony. The point where the curls of the forehead meet the volute of the ear has been rendered with an obvious conceit. The same is true of the concentric movement of the braids like thick pearls which fall on the shoulders. I find this marked preference for design values over sculptural, a little surprising.

We are all agreed on the comparisons imposed with regard to many of the characteristic traits of this work. First of all we think of the Tenea kouros: the same slenderness, the same harmonious symmetry of somatic outlines above and below the waist, the same central position of the umbilicus equidistant from the top of the thoracic arch and the pubis, the same shape of the overfold of the muscles at the knee. Then it recalls the Anavyssos kouros, in the curved depression underlining the abdomen and in the rendering of the umbilicus. Lastly, it can be compared with kouros Ptoon NM 12, mainly for the shape of the plinth and the feet belonging to it: the position of the feet, next to one another, their morphology, the relatively long toes, the manner (rare) of their placement a little behind the edge of the plinth, which is the same oval shape; on all those points the comparison is characteristic.

And how could one not think of Ptoon NM 12 kouros again for the general expression of the face and for the type of divergent spirals on the forehead in combination with the pearlshaped braids? However, the sections of curls which fill the intervals between the locks on the brow can be seen again, with greater precision, on the Kea kouros, and on the Getty the reticulum of the mass of hair is monotonously regular and the inflation behind the nape of the neck, under the pressure of the fillet, creates vertical ringlets which seem to penetrate the upper part of the back, instead of adapting absolutely to the curvature of the shoulders (I know of very few examples exactly like it).

Since the Getty kouros can be compared at once with the Tenea kouros, the Anavyssos kouros and the Ptoon NM 12 kouros, it has been considered an eclectic work. One must admit that it is difficult to date by the usual criteria and, furthermore, it is impossible to attribute to a characteristic regional style, that is to determine its provenance, apart perhaps from the kind of marble from which it is fashioned. The material resembles the dolomitic marble of Thasos. And yet the study of dolomitic marbles has evidently not progressed sufficiently for one to be certain that there were no other quarries outside Thasos in antiquity. Nor, I think, has a catalogue of Greek works in such material been compiled. Thus, when the Ludovisi and the Boston thrones are cited, or the Mozia ephebe, these are works found in Italy or in Magna Graecia and since the authenticity of at least one is dubious, we remain sceptical.

When archaeologists have doubts they resort to the "oracle" of the physicists. Alas, I am not competent to discuss with them "de-dolomitization" as incontrovertible proof of the authenticity of the Getty statue. I would just like to know if this phenomenon has been observed and studied on sculptures or architectural members, primarily on Thasos, recovered from excavations and thus certainly ancient.

As I await an answer, I shall confess my reservations. I have the impression that this wonderful work, more heteroclite than eclectic in style, is a modern creation. Indeed I would name it "The Kouros" and I would be happy to gaze upon it in the World's Fair at Seville as a smiling and robust allegory of eternal Hellas.

Georgios Dontas

THE GETTY KOUROS: A LOOK AT ITS ARTISTIC DEFECTS AND INCONGRUITIES

In the controversy regarding the authenticity of the Getty kouros a factor that must be taken into account is, in my opinion, the unfavourable feeling it arouses at the very first glance. In fact the spectator can make no sentimental contact with the work, and no matter how much and how long he tries to get rid of this first feeling he will not succeed, the statue will leave him cold. And this is a very serious defect. However, since the search for the authenticity of a work of art should not be limited to feelings and subjective criteria but requires definite arguments, I shall put forward some of the most salient defects and incongruities in the field of stylistic analysis. These, I believe, will exclude any possibility of doubt that the work is a fake.

To start with, a very serious defect is the way the hair meets the flesh on the back. Here, indeed, the "beads" disappear awkwardly on contact with the body; one needs only compare how the same junction is effected on either the Anavyssos kouros or that of Kea, two kouroi considered to be the contemporaries of the Getty kouros (the former being also stylistically related). In these statues the "beads" diminish in size as they approach the flesh and rest gently on it, they do not just disappear as here. One should also compare how on these kouroi (and on yet earlier ones) the mass of hair descending to meet the body on the back, lies organically, naturally, whereas here the mass of hair remains stiff, contrary to its organic nature, and its "beads" are "impenetrable" to the eye.

The face of the Getty kouros presents similar defects. The mouth has the Archaic smile, but its expression is forced and does not correspond to the other facial features: the eyes which are virtually horizontal, the cheeks which are flat, deprived of any internal tension and not associated with the smile. The cheeks convey no sense of the skeleton underneath, in contrast to the Munich kouros, where the visage bears some resemblance to that of the Getty kouros (with the exception of the hair).

Whereas the feet of the Acropolis kouros and those of Ptoon 12, supposed to be contemporary with the Getty, have long, aristocratic, toes on which the bone structure is emphasized, here the feet are more realistic, more fleshy, as was usual only later. Also the long axis has here been balanced to a considerable degree by a naturalistic widening of the foot and the outlines are much more fluid, as on late works. The "step" of the foot is likewise more naturalistic as one expects on later works. How then can the presence of a trait that appeared after 530 B.C. (the proposed date of the kouros) be justified?

The corporeal vigour of the Getty kouros does not emanate convincingly from the entire body, as on the Anavyssos kouros, but essentially only from its thighs. The buttocks are small and firm when seen from the sides and the upper arms are completely flaccid and smooth. The whole body lacks the vital axis which marks all works of art without exception, even the most insipid, the pose is wooden, hesitant, not free.

In conclusion, elements from various earlier styles have indeed been used in the Getty kouros, and very adroitly, but some traits of later times have also slipped in. Above all, however, the work suffers from the lack of a deeper sense of organic cohesion, it lacks, so to speak, the central organic "meaning" and the vital "breath" that are so characteristic of genuine Greek artistic creations.

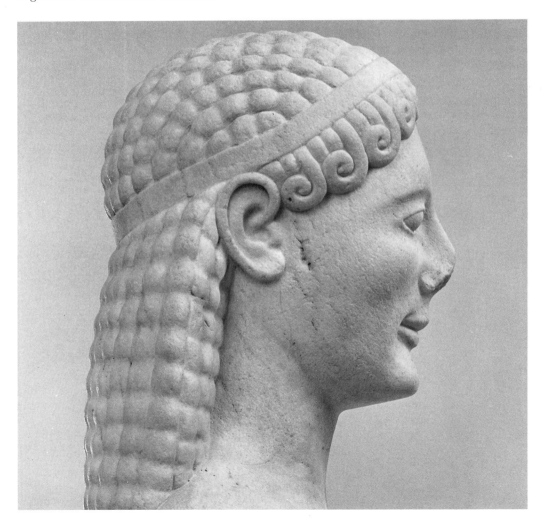

Helmut Kyrieleis

CONCERNING THE GETTY KOUROS

Adolf Furtwängler once remarked that it would be far worse to characterize an ancient work of art as a fake than to be misled by a very good imitation. It is in this spirit, which is not, of course, understood as a directive to museum directors, that we approach a basic point of archaeological recognition which also concerns us here. As archaeologists we have been taught and have become accustomed to regard the authenticity of our sources as given. This is the starting point of archaeological inquiry. Here, however, this hypothesis, is doubted.

The dating of a work on the basis of stylistic criteria, that is to take form as the subject of documentation, is, undoubtedly, a very important enterprise. The analysis of form should, in the absence of other evidence, furnish the decisive criteria for the dating of a work. At first one could compare the dilemma facing us with another frequently appearing problem, that is whether a work is an original of the Classical or Hellenistic period or a Roman copy. In this case too there is the difficulty of recognizing the specific style of the period of a sculpture on the basis of the most detailed possible analysis of form. This happens, of course, provided one has confidence in the truth of ancient fundamental principles which our comparing eye has formed.

When the question, ancient masterpiece or extremely successful fake, is posed, the ground slips from under our feet, since the very criteria on which the judgement will be made are themselves the subject of suspicion. Of one thing we can be certain: a really good "faker" is as cognizant of these criteria as the archaeologist. Furthermore, when he succeeds in fashioning forms which appear genuine, then he uses precisely those means with which the archaeologist is wont to construct his arguments. Even considerable experience gained from studying Archaic sculpture is only of minimal help to the archaeologist in confronting the difficulties arising from the suspicion that a work is a fake. For here holds true that which holds for human relationships: when trust is shaken, even once, that is, when suspicion is born, then one can no longer rely on anything. Henceforth everything is dubious or suspect. In the case of the dilemma, genuine or fake, this means respectively: once the shadow of suspicion is cast, known forms easily provide indications of deceptive imitation of familiar models, and unusual or original traits in a work, which would be considered particularly valuable in a creation above reproach, become *argumentum ex silentio* against authenticity. Precisely because there is no general canon in Archaic sculpture and the works of this period display individually remarkable differences and similarities in the most diverse details, the observation that this or that detail does not appear in other works in the same manner or that it is reminiscent of this or that work, cannot constitute a decisive argument. Who among us would, for instance, consider the Volomandra kouros or the Milani kouros in Florence above suspicion if these works had appeared in the same dim light as surrounds the Getty kouros on account of its murky provenance? Without secure evidence of provenance the usual criteria of stylistic analysis for works or problems of this kind cease to operate. The archaeologist must either become a criminologist and collect specific pieces of suspicious evidence or rely subjectively on his instinct or experience. I do not doubt that the sense of quality, which is based on experience and the practised eye, can constitute a serious guide. However, as a scholar, one should be able, beyond a feeling that the work is good or bad, be able to enumerate and to demonstrate those points which, ostensibly and objectively, are against the authenticity of the work.

I admit that, although I have a very unpleasant feeling about this kouros, I am unable to discover this kind of evidence in its partial forms. The peculiar formal eclecticism, which Marion True discusses above and which prompted some scholars to consider this work a fake, can be paralleled with analogous phenomena in Late Archaic art. Similarly I was not particularly convinced by Jeffrey Spier's comparison, in the *Burlington Magazine*, of the kouros with a known fake, for on that work, in the rendering of the hair, for example, the modern "touch" is obvious, something which is not, in my opinion, the case on the Getty kouros.

I consider Marion True's and the Getty Museum's initiative in holding this colloquium brave and praiseworthy. However, concerning the authenticity of the kouros, for the reasons explained above and despite repeated examination of it, I would not like to express an opinion. I have had too little exposure to spurious works to be able to express a responsible opinion. Perhaps there is the possibility of objectively establishing its authenticity, using the methods of the positive sciences, for instance. Nevertheless the suspicion remains and this is due exclusively to the fact that we are not certain about the sculpture's provenance. It will be difficult to remove the stigma of the counterfeit from a work such as this as long as its exact provenance remains unconfirmed. In my opinion this case indicates that museums, as public foundations, misinterpret their mission when they acquire objects of dubious provenance and have to conceal from scholarship the most important item of information, where the work comes from.

Ismini Trianti

FOUR KOUROI IN ONE?

Scholars have devoted much attention to the Getty kouros since its purchase by the Getty Museum in 1985. This is only to be expected for a new, impressive and intact statue of unknown provenance. However, the statue has also been the focus of study because it presents several problems not usually concentrated in one work. There are idiosyncrasies in the rendering of details, which deviate from the naturalistic conception towards which kouroi tend, and the erosion of its surface is peculiar and may well have been induced artificially to mask imperfections and the marks of modern tools. The kouros is of white Thasian marble, which is not common outside the Thasos region and northern Greece in Archaic times and would be justified only if the work displayed traits of a Parian-Thasian atelier. Not only is this not the case, the work cannot in fact be accommodated in any specific workshop group. Lastly, it features earlier and later developing elements spanning an interval of at least thirty years.

My observations concern two of the above issues: the idiosyncrasies in the rendering of details and the assigning of the kouros to an atelier.

The form and rendering of the ears may be regarded as idiosyncratic, not merely because they are positioned at differing heights but because each is different in conception: the left one is oblong, the right round. Likewise idiosyncratic is the very regular ovoid plinth, uniformly worked with a claw chisel on the lateral faces and the upper surface.

The rendering of the sternum and chest with lax planes and an inelegant, harsh vertical groove, which is repeated on the spine, reveal the sculptor's inability to grasp the organic structure of the body. Likewise inorganic are the grooves defining the shoulders, the left one of which is too long and interrupts the outline of the thorax. Great confusion is observed in the hands, which rest on the thighs with a thin, transitional, intervening mass of marble which also continues onto the forearm. The top of the muscles above the knee is not correctly rendered, while the rendering of the top lip and especially the absence of the groove below the middle of the nose constitute a deviation from a naturalistic conception.

The Getty kouros cannot be characterized as a provincial work. Although it has been carved from Thasian marble, the only element related to surviving Thasian or Parian works is the type of the curls of its coiffure. These are beaded with triangular ends on the back, a characteristic so common on kouroi that it is not particularly helpful. However, both in shape and modelling, the helicoid curls on the forehead are appropriate to island workshops and closely resemble the Kea kouros which is considered to be from the western Cycladic atelier. The syntax of the details of the torso, front and back, in a way reproduces details of the Attic kouros from Anavyssos. However, the sloping shoulders are encountered on the Tenea kouros and on small bronze figurines designated as Corinthian. The plinth and feet resemble those which have been attributed to the Ptoon 12 kouros, which some scholars regard as an Attic work, others as Boeotian, and Ducat as eclectic, of Cycladic style with a mixture of Naxian and Parian traits.

It is apparent from the foregoing remarks that traits of several ateliers coexist in the Getty kouros: the Attic, the Corinthian, the western Cycladic as well as a school that may be Cycladic, as expressed in the Ptoon 12 kouros.

Given the difficulties arising from the lack of stylistic consistency, the Getty kouros has been considered eclectic. For this same reason Megara is cited as its possible provenance in a manual published in 1990. Theoretically the geographical location of Megara would seem to favour influences from both Corinth and Attica as well as from Boeotia and the islands.

Wherever the term eclectic is used for works of this period, however, it implies the existence of a workshop base which has been subjected to strong influences. For the Getty kouros the workshop base is absent and no assimilated workshop influences are visible. In my opinion a selection and reproduction of sections of specific, intact Archaic kouroi was made for fashioning this work: the Tenea, Kea, Anavyssos and Ptoon 12 kouroi. The hair is a combination of Ptoon and Kea, the face Ptoon and Anavyssos, the shoulders and hands Tenea and, lastly, the plinth and feet are of Ptoon 12, which are the only ones to have survived intact and which have been virtually copied. Whereas the claw has been used over the entire surface of the plinth of the Getty kouros, top and sides, traces of its use are confined to a small section of the plinth of Ptoon 12, in front of the right foot, most probably associated, as on Aristodikos, with the placement of the statue on its base.

Perhaps the Getty kouros is, after all, an eclectic work, though not ancient but modern.

Angelos Delivorrias

CONCERNING THE PROBLEM OF THE AUTHENTICITY OF A STATUE

The questions hanging over the much-discussed Getty kouros not only pertain to the relationship between the apparent and the actual time of its creation, but also to the relationship between the apparent and the actual place of its origin. Space and time are, however, two values more generally dependent on the relativity and indefinability of things. The same holds also for the concepts of truth and falsehood, which are governed by an elasticity, relating to the more or less objective or subjective weight of the criteria of intellect and knowledge. To the above one should add the epistemological problem which is, in any case, presented by the continually mutating relationship between the observer and the observed – the elusive object continually escaping, through the dimensions of space and time. Thus it is evident that the theoretical-philosophical approach to these whole issues presupposes a far more extensive development than is possible in the two pages, in which I shall attempt to squeeze the already compressed views expounded in my ten-minute paper at the Colloquium.

Quite apart from the quality of its marble, the sculpture under study could never have been carved in Attica. It lacks that density of composition which, even from Early Archaic times, made its indelible mark on Attic art. It also lacks the sharpness of outline which is the distinguishing trait of Corinthian art, just as it lacks the island inspiration that infuses those Boeotian creations which managed to liberate themselves from the wooden schematization of their origins. The attributing of the work to a putative atelier at Megara cannot be supported by serious arguments. Moreover, since it is worked in Thasian marble, its stylistic dependence on the Thasian, or at least the Parian, artistic tradition would seem to be more probable, or rather more expected. And yet, try as we may, it is difficult to perceive even remote island impulses in the modelling of its form. Therefore, the kouros' authenticity can only be supported by the forced association of two assumptions: the unconfirmed export of Thasian marble in Archaic times and the statue's execution in an as yet unknown artistic centre of the period. I consider it superfluous to emphasize that the acceptance of these two hypotheses overturns whatever is known to date about the art of the Archaic period, just as it overturns the recognised principles of scientific method, both at the level of art history and of statistics.

Not only do I believe that the Getty kouros is a pastiche or – to use more modern vocabulary – a patchwork of stylistic allusions to several local ateliers of Archaic sculpture, I also feel the need to interpret the intuitive repulsion it arouses in me. Among the serious, scientifically documented reasons for condemning an artistic creation, it is, of course, difficult to include qualities maligned because of their metaphysical nature, though I personally would argue that these derive from the distillate of lived experience, which should not be dismissed lightly. Nevertheless, to prove the validity of intuition would necessitate investigating its chemical composition, as well as providing the author with more paper on which to develop his inquiries.

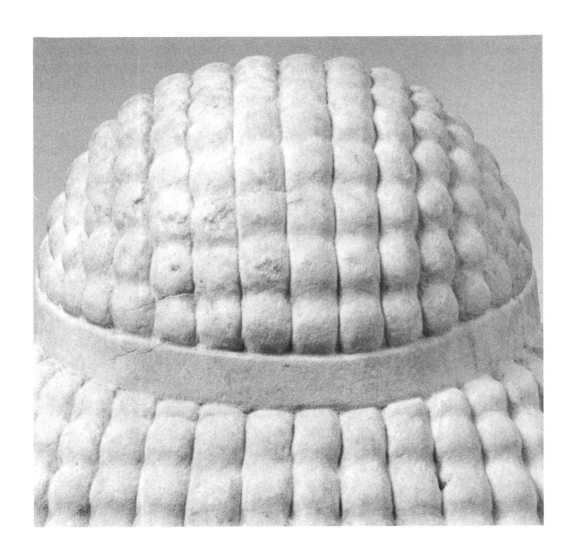

Ilse Kleemann

ON THE AUTHENTICITY OF THE GETTY KOUROS

In a television report, entitled *The Fine Art of Faking it*, screened in the USA on December 17, 1991, which included also the Getty kouros and which was seen by the speaker on April 19 this year in Germany, Dr. Marion True summarized the situation as follows: "Neither art history nor natural science can give a definite answer to the question of authenticity, because stylistic observations tend to be subjective, but also the results of natural science are not as safe as had been thought."

This is certainly correct. However, in addition to these two approaches there is still a third approach – that of the objective and thorough analysis of form: the observation of given shapes as facts and of the formal elements used in Archaic works of art, leading to an understanding of the purpose and meaning of these formulae.

The question may be asked "Is not style also form?," for which reason the term "form," as understood here, needs definition.

The formulae of Archaic art are the same all over the Greek world, from Asia Minor to Sicily, and do not change during the Archaic period proper. One may therefore speak of "form as such." Yet, the Archaic formulae were applied in different landscapes. That rendering may be called "form as style." The relationship between "form as such" and "form as style" can be compared with that of standard language and dialect. Form as such is the basic pattern and precedes form as style. The latter depends on the former. The sculptors learned the basic patterns in the workshops and applied them according to their provenance and training, as Parians, Naxians, Boeotians etc.

The faithful observation of form should be accompanied by practical means developed from the respective situations (in response to Konstantinos Romaios' demand for a more precise analysis of the works of Greek art). The practical means used by the speaker have been described in her publication *Early Movement*, vol. I, 1984.

Alas, the means employed by the speaker have been confused with recent, more sophisticated devices as well as being viewed with reserve as mere techniques, unsuitable for the intercourse with works of art. The means in question do not belong to this horizon, however. They are simple and spontaneous and would have been the same at any time. Thus, while at the Colloquium the speaker's studies were included in the "technical features" session, the results would never have been achieved with tools alone. Both together, the patient viewing and reviewing of the shapes and the supporting use of instruments will lead to a closer understanding.

The method of studying form in the way described does not only apply to kouroi – although the whole inquiry started from the Aristodikos kouros in the National Museum, Athens – for it cannot be expected that the formal expression of a period is limited to only one type of figure. So, in the course of time research was extended to other figures, such as korai, gods, sphinxes etc.

The outcome of these efforts was what might be called a "canon of form" used by Archaic artists. This canon is like a code that had to be deciphered gradually in order to be read. Archaic art holds a certain order of composition and with it goes a code of formulae that can be observed and defined. These are not accidental but are evidence of principles found in all Archaic figures. To suppress or ignore them is to deprive the ancient artist of what he meant to say. The difficulty in identifying these formulae is due to the historical situation of Archaic art as a period of transition between the strict frontality of the old Oriental cultures and the free movement in Classical times.

The "code" makes it possible to enter the Archaic mode of imagination in rendering movement. It opens up a new approach, in fact a new field of learning. To work with these formulae gives the viewer an untiring sense of discovery as well as a deepened aesthetic satisfaction.

The Getty kouros was studied from these viewpoints. The idea was that after many years of work it should be possible to resolve the issue of its authenticity one way or the other. The whole of the research had to stand the test.

The result is that the kouros is consistent with the kouros type in general and also with the special variation to which he belongs. This can be illustrated here by reference to the plinth and the feet.

The kouros as a type should always turn to the advanced leg, which is the left. When he is required to turn left, there is no problem. But he cannot turn to the right directly. When this is required the sculpture is set on the base in an oblique direction to the right. The angle at which the figure is rotated on the base depends on the figure's position in relation to the Hieron – temple, altar etc. – for, being a dedication, he should turn towards the godhead and not towards the visitor. This is confirmed by figures found *in situ*.

That the Getty kouros is of the latter variation can be seen *inter alia* from his plinth and feet, which are one of the strongest pieces of evidence of its authenticity.

The plinth and feet were measured by the Getty conservator Jerry Podany in the fall of 1990. At the Colloquium four large plates with drawings on a scale of 1:1 were exhibited. Plates I-II showed three versions of the plinth and feet of the Getty kouros, accompanied by respective photographs of the feet. A typical plinth in Thebes was also added. Plate III showed the left foot and plinth of the Sounion kouroi A, B and C. Plate IV showed the kouros in New York: the overall plan with plinth and feet plus the contours of the body, in the oblique stance of the figure to the right on the ancient base, i.e. *in situ*, as well as the feet on the plinth only, striding forward as in a normal museum mounting.

One of the most significant phenomena with regard to this kouros type is the way in which the feet stand on the plinth along their longitudinal axes. While the right foot has a straight axis, that of the left one is broken or bent so that the foremost part of the foot does not point outwards but is parallel with the step axis of the figure. This is done in effort to effect a turn to the right. This variation of the kouros "turning to the right," with a broken axis of the left foot and an oval or rhomboid plinth, is found not only in the Getty kouros and the examples shown in the plates, but also in the Melos kouros and that from Tenea – indeed the majority of known kouroi.

As a substitute for the plates, an idea of the *in situ* stance of the kouros, "orientated to the right," can be gained from vol. I of *Early Movement* (p. 93, pl. 35 and fig. 27, showing the base, plinth and feet of the Charopinos kouros in Delphi – the axis of the left foot at the heel should be drawn symmetrically to it and will then appear broken).

As to the torso with head which was also exhibited, during the Colloquium, this can be read as a fake. It is a gross imitation of the kouros from Paros in the Louvre, MND 888, Richter, *Kouroi* no. 116, figs. 356-358, with irregularities in the hair which are quite contrary to the code. They show how a faker works. No such mistakes are to be found on the Getty kouros, which instead displays a masterful rendering of the formulae. Once these are more intimately known the phantom of an ingenious faker will disappear.

The Getty kouros can well be placed in the development of sixth century B.C. sculpture. The speaker would like to put him about 540 B.C., that is to say more or less contemporary with the kouros NM 12 from the Ptoon, and in the landscape of Attica, in a remote relation to the Sounion Group.

The conclusions of this paper were confirmed by several days close study of the actual figure after its arrival in Athens. More may be said in a monograph on the kouros, which might also serve as an introduction to volume II of *Early Movement*.

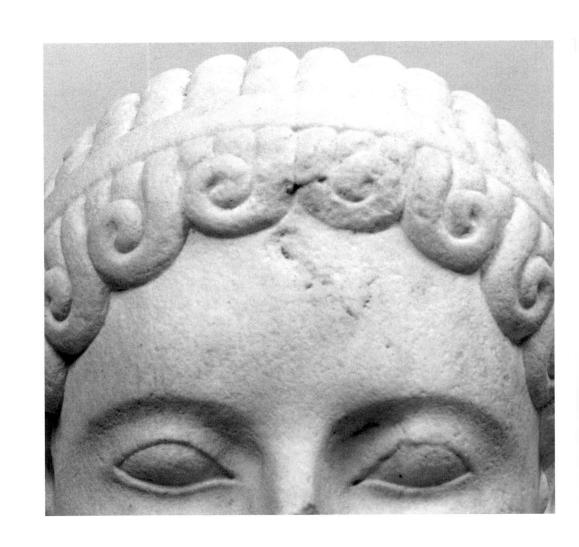

Eleanor Guralnick

MEASUREMENTS AND PROPORTIONS OF THE GETTY KOUROS

The Getty kouros was measured in 1984, 1986 and 1991. The Basel torso was measured in 1990 and 1991. A corpus of measurements for 25 well-preserved kouroi has been collected, analyzed and published over the years since 1968. Several different analytical methods have been developed to study the measurements and the proportions of statues. Only a few of the results will be highlighted here, comparisons of the Getty and Basel statues with each other, with 25 other previously studied kouroi, and with real human beings.

A z-score profile is a graphic presentation which compares each anatomical descriptor of a statue with that same descriptor for a perfectly average man. The statue profile is created by connecting its z-scores in a standard sequence. Profiles may be compared. Human data for the calculation of the z-scores comes from the 1963 NATO *Anthropometric Study of Greek, Italian and Turkish Air Force Personnel*.

The profiles of the Getty and Basel statues are dissimilar. Basel is significantly broader and thicker than Getty. Its head is shorter in proportion to its body length from the top of the knee to the top of the head, and thus its body is longer. The profiles of Getty, Anavyssos, Munich, Keratea and Kea, follow the same general pattern of narrow waist, with head height barely within the normal human range. However, the Getty statue is more slender in the shoulders, chest, waist and hips, and has a more compressed torso. The Getty profile is closer to those of a group of statues conventionally dated slightly earlier, Tenea, Melos and Volomandra. Its waist width is almost the same as those of Tenea and Volomandra and the basic profile pattern is very similar. The Athens 12 profile is the closest match to the Getty's, but the Getty work is not an identical copy of Athens 12 nor of any other kouros. It is unique and distinctive in its proportions. Athens 12 is a member of the same chronological group as Anavyssos, Munich and Kea, although it is stylistically distinctive, illustrating the variety of sculptural conceptions represented within any one brief period of Archaic sculpture. The similarity of the Getty profile to profiles of the Tenea-Melos Group and to a select number of the Anavyssos-Munich Group suggest it may reflect a transitional conception combining features of both. Its closest relationships are with a group of related statues which span a relatively broad chronological band. If its proportional cousins span so generous a number of years, it is not surprising that its stylistic affinities have a broad span. Chronological development systems are our modern inventions intended to aid in understanding the broad, general development trends of Archaic sculpture. In antiquity there were, no doubt, creative sculptors carving in advanced, innovative ways, simultaneously with old fashioned sculptors who rejected the new and conformed to conventional approaches and still others who combined the conventions of their training with some innovation. Our chronological systems should not blind us to the hesitant and tentative nature of evolution in style and proportion. Richter intended us to pay attention to exceptions as well as to the substantiations of her framework for the appreciation of general trends in Archaic Greek sculpture.

The more that is learned about the proportions of Archaic Greek kouroi, the more persuasive is the idea that each kouros is a unique interpretation of a basic, broadly accepted idea of how to idealize from the human form to create a work of sculptural art. Idealizations changed through time and reflected differing local and/or individual interpretations. This uniqueness of each Archaic Greek statue contributes to the difficulty of judging a piece without provenance. When surface style and proportions are inconsistent, as they are in the Basel torso, we have good reason to question authenticity. When style and proportions are concordant, as they are for the Getty kouros, we have less reason to suspect the product of a modern sculptor.

The disparity between the slender upper torso of the Getty kouros and its very heavily developed thighs is explained by comparisons with modern athletes. Each of the medalists in the 1960 Olympic Games at Rome has been photographed standing in a standard pose. The results were published in 1964 as *Anthropometric Studies of Olympic Athletes*. Comparison of the Getty kouros with the Olympians revealed that it shares a specialized body type with a very successful athlete, V. Gorayev, medalist in the triple-jump competition. Gorayev has a very slender upper torso, highly developed *trapezium*, and very heavily muscled thighs and calves. If a specialized athletic body type provides a model for the kouros, then that model is the body of a jumping champion. The Getty's kouros rather narrow shoulders have parallels among authentic kouroi. Athens 10 has even narrower shoulders, and Merenda, Melos and Kea have only slightly broader ones.

The proportions and design of the Getty kouros are within the mainstream for kouroi, with no anomalies to single it out from the body of 25 others studied. In fact, several others are substantially more singular in their proportions (Rambearer, Dermys and Kitylos, for example). Its proportions are not based on a model selected from among the other examples of the type. Rather, it is distinctive and individual, as are all other kouroi.

Stelios Triantis

TECHNICAL AND ARTISTIC DEFICIENCIES OF THE GETTY KOUROS

All the known Archaic kouroi conform to canons and all display singularities. These singularities, few or many, small or large, do not overturn the general canons; they classify an Archaic kouros in an atelier cycle and if two kouroi from the same atelier cycle have singularities in common, then we think they may have been made by the same artist. Subject to the canons are: (a) the technique of removing the marble from the outside inwards in mantles, (b) the use of measurements and patterns, and (c) the tools of the period and the manner in which they were used.

Since we see the kouros finished, we have nothing to say about the technique followed in its sculpting and we assume it was made in the usual way for its time. I must, however, point out that, though I searched most carefully, nowhere did I observe points where one would expect the front and the back face to join – down the length of the arms, on the inside part of the upper arms and on the corresponding point of the statue's torso. Usually two peaks are created at these junctures, more pronounced on the earlier statues and gradually diminishing over the years, being virtually smoothed off on the last kouroi of the Archaic period.

As far as the patterns are concerned, the fact that the Getty kouros has ears of two different types, with regard to their general outline, means that the artist used two different patterns or none at all.

The measurements appear to be canonical.

On account of the considerable erosion, traces of tools have disappeared from virtually the entire surface of the kouros and I cannot say whether this has been smoothed with emery. The only visible tool marks are discernible in the recesses of the sculpture, the only places they have been preserved. These are:

A visible trace as if from a fine point on the vertical cleft separating the buttocks, between the fingers down their length, as well as on the outlines of the curls.

Small V-shaped traces of a slope chisel at the top of the cleft between the buttocks and on the armpits.

Traces of a point on the arches of the soles of the feet and at random on all faces of the plinth.

Traces of a claw chisel on the faces, the upper surface and the underside of the plinth, as well as faint marks on the surface of the left calf and *metatarsus*.

There are drill marks only in the two nostrils of the broken nose.

The few tool marks remaining after the marked erosion of the statue, less on the surface but untouched in its deeper parts, are not consonant with its execution in accordance with the habits of Archaic sculpting. Indeed the fine point, slope chisel and claw chisel, popular tools in later times and up to the present day, could be said to first appear on statues at the end of the Archaic period. However, no sculptor of kouroi would hollow out with a fine point, nor incise outlines with this tool, which in our case resembles a running drill.

I also note as worthy of attention that the plinth differs from sixth-century plinths, which are restricted in area round the soles of the feet. At that time, moreover, the plinth also played the role of a tenon which, with lead cast in the cavity of the base, held the statue upright. This plinth looks as if it has been made to maintain the statue erect on its own, without being inserted in a base. One would expect its walls to be vertical or diminishing slightly downwards and the underside to be more smoothly worked, to facilitate the flow of moulten lead.

Concerning the artistic rendering of the statue, I observe that there are weaknesses, I would dare say defects, in individual details, although as a whole it presents an impressive image. The artists of the Archaic period paid serious attention to human nature in all their works and, despite abstractionist and geometrical renderings, always endeavoured not to contravene the canons of the human body. I regard as unnatural renderings: (a) the deficient mass of the *rectus abdominis* muscle and the line defining it from one armpit to the other, (b) the inflation of the ribs below the breast on the *latissimus dorsi* muscle, (c) the joining of the three muscles at the armpit, the *deltoid*, the *biceps brachii* and the *pectoralis major*, which is lax and lower than the correct position, (d) the dividing line on the sternum, from the xiphisternum to the throat, which is very deep, (e) the modelling of the thigh muscles overall and in their ligament at the knee. Lastly, I consider the rendering of the fingers unnatural, particularly the little one, bent at the last phalanx, which is deficient in volume and pointed and, instead of resting in the palm, is displaced to its outer edge.

In the light of the foregoing remarks, I conclude that it is difficult to include the Getty kouros in the statuary of the sixth century B.C.

Peter Rockwell

ARCHAIC CARVING TECHNIQUE AND THE GETTY KOUROS

B y way of introduction to my commentary, I would like to say that from reading the literature on the subject of ancient sculpting I have the impression that the authors think that marble carving technology is a much simpler subject than it actually is to the practitioner. By neglecting or simplifying aspects of carving they have created an intellectually satisfying picture that has little relation to either the reality of work or the evidence of the unfinished carvings. As a corollary, one would assume from the literature that we understand pretty thoroughly the technical practices of Archaic Greek carvers. As a carver, I am not at all certain that I know how and with what tools the Archaic marble sculptor worked. I do think, however, that from about 550 to 470 B.C. the technology was well-developed and some of it differed in important ways from our own.

The Getty kouros exhibits four techniques that are characteristic of Archaic technology and alien to both modern and most of medieval and ancient technology:

(1) The figure was carved lying prone. Archaic kouroi had to be carved prone because there were no supports at the ankles to prevent the marble from breaking at that point. Both the Thasos rambearer and the unfinished youth from Naxos show that the figures were roughed out this way. This characteristic is unique to Archaic carving.

(2) There is one piece of evidence that the spaces between the arms and the body were carved without using the drill. Under the right arm, there is a place where the form of the torso seen from the back does not match with that from the front. This is a characteristic problem of opening spaces from two sides without the use of the drill.

It is normally presumed that these spaces were executed with the aid of a drill. However, neither the Athens unfinished kouros nor the Thasos rambearer nor the Taranto kore show signs of a drill used to excavate such spaces. The torso of Sombrotidas in the Syracuse Museum shows, in an unfinished portion between the left arm and body, the most probable technique. It is the same technique that can be observed in unfinished Egyptian granite carvings. The carver carefully outlines the space, working slowly in from both back and front without the use of the drill. This technique risks leaving precisely the sort of line found on the Getty kouros.

(3) The details of the figure, ears, hair, and eyes are isolated as separate, three-

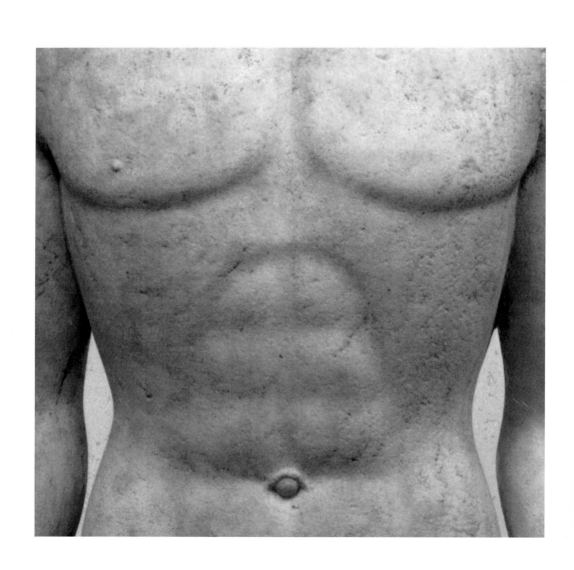

dimensional geometric entities before any carving of the details within them is executed. We have several examples of this in unfinished works including the ears of the Thasos piece, the privates of the Athens kouros, the ears of the Munich head from Naxos and the drapery of the Taranto kore.

A comparison between the right ears of the Getty kouros and the Getty fake are interesting in this respect. The ear of the Getty kouros is three-dimensionally separate from the hair around it and the face. The ear of the fake, however, is an extension of the same form as the hair behind it, whereas at the front it slopes into the cheek. Therefore, although it is visually an ear, it is formally part of the hair sloping to the face. The Getty kouros ear is both visually and formally distinct.

(4) The direction of the blow of the tool in relation to the surface of the stone on the Getty kouros is either vertical or at a high angle. The tooth chiselling of the base clearly exhibits lines perpendicular to the movement of the chisel which are characteristic of carving when the tool is either a form of an axe or is held at a steep angle to the plane of the stone. The same sort of marks are visible on the surface of the Munich head and the Taranto kore. The shapes of the components of the hair, as well as the spaces between them, show the use of a flat chisel that is held at a steep angle.

It is something of a conundrum whether these marks on the unfinished pieces were made by a hammer and chisel or a carving axe, though the axe is likely.

It is extremely difficult for a modern carver to reproduce axe marks with any consistency with a hammer and chisel. Carvers in Europe have not used axes for carving marble since the early sixteenth century. For a modern carver to produce the effect of the tool use on the hair of the Getty kouros would take a radical retraining in tool use. For the Archaic carver it was normal.

All of the above technical characteristics imply a series of problems with which no modern carver is familiar. It is not just a change in tool use. It is a change in one's whole attitude toward the act of carving.

There are two interesting characteristics of the Getty kouros which set it far apart from the Getty fake. First is the consistency of the technique. Not only are there no technical anomalies that strike the eye on first view, but even after several days of observation there are still none. Like the Archaic carvers, the carver followed a technique that gives all the signs of a well-established and careful methodology. In a very artisan-like fashion, the tool use remains the same whatever the detail. Modern carvers, like the fake carver, are much more likely to adapt their technique flexibly to the type of detail being carved.

The second characteristic is the lack of signs of any attempt to conceal or obfuscate tool use. Within the limits of the weathering of the surfaces, the tool marks are consistently clear. In contrast, the fake shows considerable variety of acid treatment which varies the surface and tries, unsuccessfully, to obscure modern tool use.

If the Getty kouros is a fake of the last 50 years, it is a completely anomalous one. Since the time of Alceo Dossena, the direction of modern faking seems to be toward the creation of heavily damaged pieces with a maximum of surface treatment with acids and other materials. One purpose or effect of these treatments is to erase the telltale signs of modern technique from the surface. The Getty kouros shows no sign of these techniques. It is quite easy to read its surfaces.

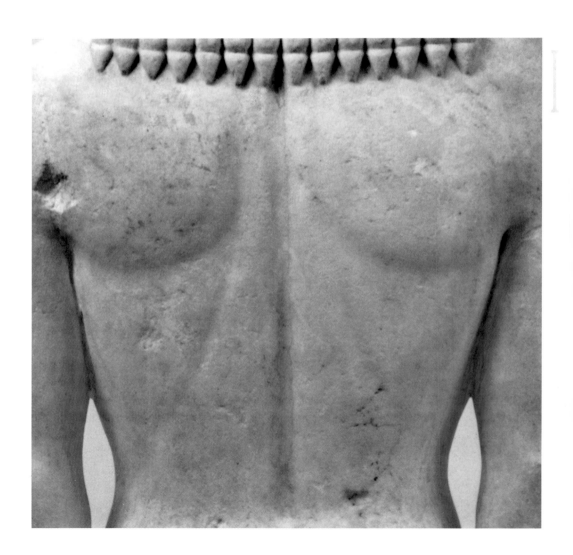

Jerry Podany

SCIENTIFIC EXAMINATION OF THE GETTY KOUROS:
AN INTRODUCTION

In a sense the Getty kouros is an antinomy, since it seems to contradict most of our expectations about ancient art as well as modern forgery. For some years now it has confounded the efforts of scientists to provide what many expected to be provided – an absolute answer based on "pure scientific reasoning." That any scientific investigation can complete such a task and produce a single and unassailable answer is a widely held belief, perhaps especially among art historians and some archaeologists. Science, however, has limits. Limits defined by the present state of our knowledge and experience. When asked to assist in a question of authenticity, scientists can provide observations and put forward interpretations based on comparisons to what we trust as "knowns or absolutes." The tools may be quite different from those of the scholar or archaeologist: test tubes, microscopes and exotic machines rather than trowels, libraries and photographs. But the processes are quite similar. One looks at the general evidence, then focuses on the details and finally compares all of this to the "knowns." If the comparisons are substantial, a decision can be rendered. In reality, however, the process is not that simple. There exist wide variations in what are seen as "substantial comparisons" both among scientists and scholars.

Before we examine the scientific evidence gathered over the last eight years, it is important to note that the scientist's questions can be divided into two major categories:

(1) How does a specific object compare to the sculpture, artifacts or natural products believed to be ancient and those known to be forgeries or modern productions?

(2) How did those characteristics come about? What processes, natural or induced, long- or short-term, were under way to alter the marble and leave behind the evidence observed?

The first question is limited to the availability of samples and the willingness of researchers and scholars to contribute to the investigation of ancient surfaces and known forgeries. In light of modern techniques, comparisons are relatively straight forward. The danger lies in the limited number of "knowns." Our lack of data raises the question "Is this or that characteristic always a signifier of antiquity, or does its absence always indicate a forgery?" Many features provide evidence to support either claim and many new observations have not been fully characterized as either previously unknown weathering phenomena or previously unrecorded tricks of the forger.

The latter question, "How did the evidence come to exist?," is far more difficult to answer when there appears to be no comparison to the observed features.

Unlike asking "What will the result be if a given process is carried out?" the question becomes "What was the process that led to this result?" It is a matter of working back in time and eliminating, one by one, the almost endless possibilities. This is required when the burial environment or the forger's recipes are unknown.

The investigation of the kouros addressed both questions. Scientists examined the characteristic features of long-term, natural weathering as well as forgeries and the techniques used to produce them. Regardless of how illogical some of the approaches seemed, they were all scrutinized, since only one observation, consistent with forgery and modern creation, is needed to condemn an object. The characteristics of antiquity are more varied and illusive. One can only rely on building numerous consistencies and similarities.

In this research, scientific efforts became more important for what they had proven does not exist, or did not occur, than for defining what was observed and how it came about. To date no single piece of evidence has been found that suggests or is consistent with, modern techniques of carving and patination, whether intended to deceive or not.

Most of what we observe on the kouros appears related to long-term alteration processes and to ancient surfaces. Nonetheless, there is little doubt that the surface of the sculpture is odd when compared on a macroscopic scale to the other kouroi (such as those in Athens). But after careful consideration one finds objects that present visual similarities both in color, opacity and surface texture (like those on Thasos). Hence we begin with the surface.

Initial work on the kouros began with a traditional ultra-violet examination. The UV emission did not suggest a fresh surface, nor one upon which pigment or dirt had simply been loosely washed on; rather the surface was quite complex, with variations in fluorescence of the deposits and tide lines, suggesting fluctuation in water content of surrounding material.

The surface of the sculpture and how it has or has not altered with time, and how it compares to what we expect are paramount issues. To address these issues, Dr. Stan Margolis was called to investigate the surface. Dr. Norman Herz had already established a general provenance and composition; the marble is dolomite with 8-10% calcite and its provenance is most likely the northeast section of Thasos. Although Dr. Margolis's pioneering work was interpreted as proof of a calcite crust on the surface of the sculpture, later investigation uncovered a more complex surface of calcium oxalate. Regardless, the evidence strongly suggested long-term alteration.

During the analysis, attempts were made to replicate the surface of the kouros using both known, rumored and assumed forgery techniques. In this "kitchen sink science," we recorded our steps carefully; however, the ingredients and applications were solely dictated by convenience, availability of material, time required and visual response to the treatment. If a formula was too exotic, too expensive or excessively time consuming it was dismissed after the initial trial. If the treatment did not provide a visual change that brought the sample closer to mimicking ancient patina, it was eliminated from the trials. Such practicality was the strength of this approach since it was highly unlikely that a forger's workshop would include an electron microscope or microprobe to assist in creating an altered surface seen only through such equipment. The attempts aimed at obvious visual alteration of the marble.

Acid mixtures, soils, clays, gases, organic compounds from both plant and animal sources were all tried. Samples were boiled or soaked for periods ranging from hours to months. Surfaces were treated and re-treated using their final appearance as our guide. Representative efforts from the over 200 attempts were then sent to the scientific labs for analysis to determine any necessary modifications. During these trials only a few examples appeared similar to the kouros; however, they did not maintain that similarity when scrutinized under high magnification or elemental analysis. All of the samples could be clearly traced to the techniques used. They clearly exhibited alterations due to intervention and not to natural long-term processes. Ultimately we were unsuccessful at producing any surface which matched or even closely resembled the complexities of the kouros structure. We were readily able, however, to replicate that of the forgery.

I began this contribution by warning that science cannot at this point provide absolute answers; indeed it has provided yet more questions. We have, however, learned to stretch our horizons and limit our expectations of what an ancient object should look like, as well as what a forgery can look like. And while the forgers of the future will surely continue to present challenges and surprises, I think the ancient craftsmen have even more in store for our future study.

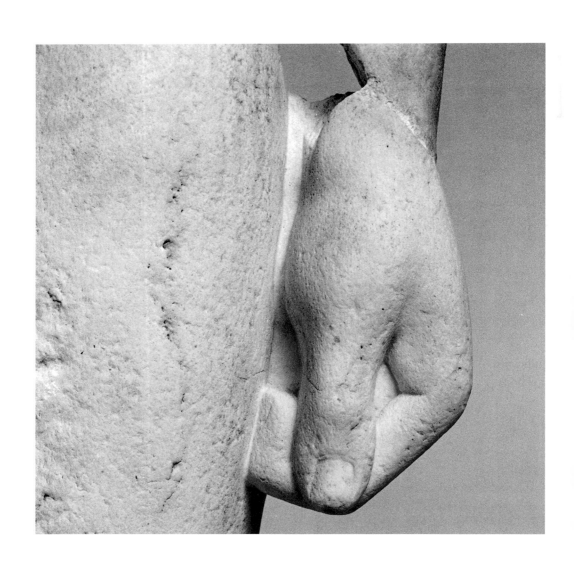

Tony Kozelj

MARBLE QUARRIES ON THE ISLAND OF THASOS
AND THE EXTRACTION OF BLOCKS IN ANTIQUITY

n the Neolithic period marble quarrying on Thasos needed little organization and the normal extraction technique made use of natural cracks resulting from erosion. Wooden crowbars were inserted into these in order to split a flagstone from the bedrock planes. These so-called quarries are mostly found in the immediate vicinity of cemeteries, where large stone slabs were used to cover and seal tombs. To facilitate transportation the sharp corners and edges of the slabs were removed with a stone hammer. One such quarry can be seen at Kastri on Thasos.

Very similar slabs were also used on the island during the Archaic period, especially for the construction of the monumental east wall of the acropolis. In the Early Archaic period squared stones for construction were either extracted as little blocks from the bedrock or as a single big block which was recut into smaller pieces by a quarryman. Archaic quarries can be seen at many locations on Thasos: the Pyrgos quarry near the Akeratos lighthouse, the Herakles quarry at Saliara and the Pholia quarry with Archaic blocks *in situ*. During Late Archaic times chisel and wedges were used together to extract a block with straight faces. If a block is cut by this method the subsequent roughing process is both easier and quicker. The residual stone chips were transported elsewhere so as not to hinder ongoing or future work in the quarry. They were often dumped in quarries which had fallen into disuse because the marble was no longer of sufficiently high quality, or thrown into the sea.

The quarries used for the extraction of kouroi in the Archaic period do not resemble those from which building material was obtained. The kouroi-quarries can be identified on the basis of the presence of "large marble fingers," as I would like to call them. Such "fingers" can be very compact and usually showed proof of their hardness since the crumbly marble had already been eaten away by erosion. Depending on the size of the "finger," one, two or even three kouroi of different dimensions, all larger than life-size, could be extracted. Good examples of this practice can be seen on Naxos and Thasos.

After a particular quarry site had been chosen for the quality of its marble, its good location etc., working areas and platforms were constructed in preparation for the extraction process.

The various techniques for extraction depended more on the quality and the eventual function of the block than on the tools used, which changed very little over time.

For the extraction of blocks for building purposes natural cracks and faults in the rock were exploited. Thus the size of the blocks, which were commonly reworked later, was determined by the spacing between the fissures. The presence of cracks on three sides is rare but allows the use of wedges. In all cases one or two trenches had to be cut first.

Extraction by heat shock was used when the rock mass had a protuberance or some prominent portion, so that all four surfaces could be worked and the size of the block to be extracted was predetermined. A guideline was cut, fire lit on either side of it and cold water thrown into the hot rock, which then split under the heat shock along the trace of the cut line. Rough hewn blocks were extracted in this way. In Egypt, where the extraction of monolithic granite obelisks demanded special techniques, red-hot bricks were used to mark the edges. When the stone was sufficiently hot it was doused with cold water in order to weaken the defined edges. Balls of dolomite, weighing about 5.5 kg., were then dropped from a man's height, causing the granite to crack to a depth of 2 to 3 cm. This is deduced from an unfinished obelisk in Egypt, 1,168 tones in weight, 41.75 m. long and 4.20 m. wide.

In extraction by hammering a furrow was first dug with a chisel and a two-handed hammer. Then the rock was cracked by the percussive effect of a tetrahedral hafted hammer.

Extraction by digging a channel and then using wedges was the most common technique in use until the age of the pneumatic hammer. The first stage consists of positioning holes to be cut for insertion of the wedges, bearing in mind the length and height required for the blocks. This operation could be repeated over a wide area of a mountainside, depending on the number of blocks to be extracted. The second stage consisted of cutting a three-sided channel to a depth corresponding to the desired size of the block. Depending on the working space and the tools available, the quarryman dug either a shallow or a deep channel.

Every year more and more new quarries for white marble are opened on the island of Thasos. The ancient quarries are increasingly in jeopardy. In opening new working faces in them many important archaeological treasures have been destroyed, though in some defunct quarries archaeological remains have been identified from the Neolithic era, as well as the Archaic, Classical, Roman, Byzantine and Medieval periods. From the ancient quarries most endangered are those located near present-day paths and country roads, since modern quarrying companies can easily come and remove "ready" blocks instead of prospecting for new caves of high-grade marble.

Frank Preusser

SCIENTIFIC EXAMINATION OF THE GETTY KOUROS

The studies carried out by a team of scientists over a period of eight years can be grouped in two main areas: (a) determination of the nature of the stone and its geographical provenance; and (b) determination of the nature and possible origin of the chemical, mineralogical and physical alterations observable on the surface of the kouros.

The stone has been identified as a well-formed dolomitic marble with an average of 10% calcite and a variety of impurities. Trace element, grain size, calcite content, strontium isotope, stable isotope and cathodoluminescence data all indicate that the stone for the sculpture was quarried somewhere along the northeast coast of Thasos, Greece. Stable isotope data were obtained from 22 ancient and four modern quarries on Thasos. The Getty kouros data fall close to those of dolomite from several ancient quarries, but do not specifically match any of the ancient or modern quarries sampled. Dolomite with stable isotope values most similar to those of the Getty kouros was obtained from a quarry that was active in the 6th century B.C., based on inscriptions and other archaeological evidence. Further field work, improved sampling statistics, and additional parameters may eventually help to identify the quarry the stone for the Getty kouros came from. However, a number of ancient quarries have been destroyed, worked out, submerged by sea level change, or have been destroyed by modern quarrying operations.

Studies of the 10 to 50 micron thick "alteration layer" on the surface of the kouros were undertaken to determine whether it has been formed naturally over the centuries and millennia or if it is the result of an "artificial patination." While preliminary analyses indicated that the layer consists of calcite formed through the process of dedolomitization, further analyses using a variety of techniques showed it to be composed mostly of calcium oxalate monohydrate (whewellite, $CaC_2O_4 \cdot H_2O$) with smaller amounts of iron oxide-rich soil and calcite. Scanning electron microscopy revealed a complex microstructure in this alteration layer. While it is possible to produce whewellite layers on dolomitic marble using oxalic acid baths, we were not able to reproduce the complexities of the kouros alteration layer.

We analyzed the kouros oxalate crust using accelerator mass spectrometry (AMS) ^{14}C dating techniques and obtained a radiocarbon age of several thousand years. While consistent with authenticity, the results are inconclusive since we were also able to obtain ^{14}C ages of several thousand years for lichen oxalate crusts and oxalate crusts prepared using dolomite marble and oxalic acid baths. The problem is not with the ^{14}C technique; it is the impossibility of knowing the exact sources of carbon in the oxalate that prevents the use of radiocarbon dating in this context.

While the scientific studies have not provided any "proof" of authenticity and most likely never will, it should be pointed out that despite the application of such a variety of technical examinations and analytical studies applied to the Getty kouros, not a single piece of evidence has turned up that would indicate that the surface alteration is of modern origin and has been produced by artificial patination. The alteration layer of the Getty kouros bears many more similarities with naturally occurring weathering crusts than with known artificially produced surfaces.

While this study has not given the ultimate answer to the question of authenticity, it has greatly advanced our understanding of weathering processes of stone and especially dolomitic marble. It has also posed many new questions that can only be addressed through a long-term international research effort. In this context it will be important to gain access to ancient marble sculptures with surfaces that have not been altered by treatments such as cleaning or surface consolidation.

Norbert S. Baer

THE ROLE OF SCIENTIFIC EVIDENCE IN ARCHAEOLOGICAL INQUIRY: THE GETTY KOUROS

Scientific examination has limits. There are certain questions to which scientists cannot hope to offer answers. For example, the Bernini problem, that is, what portion of a marble sculpture was carved and finished by the master and what portion by his assistants.

The Frye rule (formulated in *Frye vs United States*, 293 F 1013, 1014-DC, in 1923) states: "The condition for admissibility of scientific methods used to obtain evidence requires that a scientific principle must be sufficiently established to have gained acceptance in the particular field in which it belongs." Thus, new techniques, in the present case, stable isotope analysis, instrumental neutron activation analysis, dedolomitization and oxalate crust formation, should be subjected to reliability testing and critical peer review.

Two basic approaches, the static, searching for inconsistencies or anachronisms in compositional profile or technique in the object, and the dynamic approach, which examines the aging process, are used in the technical dating of artifacts. With the kouros data presented to date, we have had a thorough search for inconsistencies and a compelling examination of marble sources, i.e. the static approach. Significant data have been presented regarding the stable isotope and trace element distributions, and physical characteristics of the several quarry specimens and artifacts. Statistical analyses should be performed to assign probabilities to specific marble quarry associations. One looks forward to detailed statistical analysis of the quarry data, though the precise sources of the kouros stone and other objects may never be identified due to the destruction of ancient surfaces by current quarrying activity on Thasos.

We have also seen aspects of the dynamic approach in the examination of weathering crusts. However, statements of the sort "these weathering phenomena cannot be duplicated in the laboratory," or "in nature they take centuries or millenia" are no substitutes for geochemical rate data, i.e. microns or mm per hundred years and the certain proof that human intervention cannot accelerate these processes. While the rate problem is under active investigation, the preclusion of accelerated crust formation in some forger's brew is far more elusive.

We must also examine the working hypotheses regarding the exposure history of the kouros and ask if the observed surface phenomena are consistent with these hypotheses. For example, did the kouros experience:

  (a) Essentially continuous burial, or
  (b) Immediate exposure to lichen growth or other biological activity with oxalate crust formation in antiquity followed by burial, or
  (c) Continuous exposure in the open air, or finally
  (d) Any combination of the above followed by vigorous surface cleaning in recent times.

Jerry Podany stated that the Getty Museum had not cleaned or treated the surface, but that "the probability that it had been cleaned was high." If so, by what method – mechanical, chemical, poultice. We do not, at this time, know what this sequence of exposure, burial, cleaning was and what changes it should produce in a dolomitic surface.

Most puzzling is the previous report that "the weathered surface (of the kouros) was found to be covered with a continuous layer of calcite about 10 to 50 microns thick. The identification of calcite was confirmed both by x-ray diffraction and electron-microprobe analysis." Yet in the summary statement supplied at the Colloquium it is stated that, "subsequent analysis, however, revealed that the calcite layer was in fact calcium oxalate." It is difficult to understand how x-ray diffraction data identified calcium oxalate as calcium carbonate.

Perfect condition is not necessarily evidence of fraud. Further, a false patina is only that, it does not condemn the object. Few stone objects have entered museum collections without some surface intervention. Even today outdoor bronzes are routinely stripped to base metal by blasting with microglass beads or walnut shell fragments and then repatinated.

Stone remains the least tractable medium for technical proof of authenticity. We need substantially more research before we can with confidence accept or reject a stone sculpture on the basis of technical evidence alone.

BIBLIOGRAPHY

Marion True, A Kouros at the Getty Museum, *The Burlington Magazine*, CXXIX, no. 1006, Jan. 1987, 3-11.

Stanley Margolis, Authenticating Ancient Marble Sculpture, *Scientific American*, 260, no. 6, June 1989, 104-110.

Jeffrey Spier, Blinded by Science: the Abuse of Science in the Detection of False Antiquities, *The Burlington Magazine*, CXXXII, no. 1050, Sept. 1990, 623-631.

PARTICIPANTS

DR. MARION TRUE
Curator of Antiquities
J. Paul Getty Museum

PROF. BRUNILDE SISMONDO-RIDGWAY
Department of Classical
and Near Eastern Archaeology
Bryn Mawr College

PROF. EVELYN B. HARRISON
Institute of Fine Arts
New York University

PROF. BERNARD HOLTZMANN
University of Paris X

PROF. SIR JOHN BOARDMAN
Lincoln Professor
Oxford

PROF. VASSILIS LAMBRINOUDAKIS
Athens University

PROF. JEAN MARCADÉ
University of Paris I

DR. GEORGIOS DONTAS
President of the Archaeological
Society at Athens

PROF. DR. HELMUT KYRIELEIS
President of the German
Archaeological Institute, Berlin

DR. ISMINI TRIANTI
Curator of Antiquities
Acropolis Museum

PROF. ANGELOS DELIVORRIAS
Athens University
Director, Benaki Museum

DR. ILSE KLEEMANN
German Archaeological Institute
Athens

DR. ELEANOR GURALNICK
University of Chicago

MR. STELIOS TRIANTIS
Sculptor, National Museum
Athens

MR. PETER ROCKWELL
Sculptor, Rome

MR. JERRY PODANY
Head, Antiquities Conservation
J. Paul Getty Museum

MR. TONY KOZELJ
Ecole Française d'Athènes

DR. FRANK PREUSSER
Associate Director
The Getty Conservation Institute

PROF. NORBERT S. BAER
Hagop Kevorkian Professor
of Conservation
New York University